THE
OBERLIN BOOK OF
BANDSTANDS

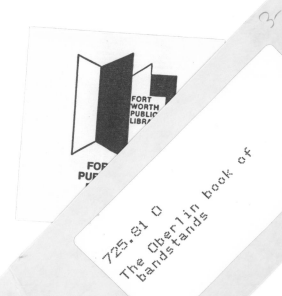

Band concert in Congress Park,
Saratoga Springs, N.Y. The band-
stand (c. 1882) was replaced in
1930–31 by a classical war
memorial, also used for concerts.
(Collection of George S. Bolster;
H. B. Settle, 1922)

THE OBERLIN BOOK OF BANDSTANDS

[S. FREDERICK STARR, EDITOR]

THE PRESERVATION PRESS

The Preservation Press
National Trust for Historic Preservation
1785 Massachusetts Avenue, N.W.
Washington, D.C. 20036

Printed in the United States of America
91 90 89 88 87   5   4   3   2   1

Library of Congress Cataloging in Publication Data

The Oberlin book of bandstands.

    Bibliography: p.
    Includes index.
1. Bandstands—United States.   2. Bandstands—Ohio—Oberlin—Competitions.   3. Architecture, Victorian—United States.   I. Starr, S. Frederick.
NA8450.O24   1987   725'.81   87-22570
ISBN 0-89133-128-X

Edited by Diane Maddex, director, and Janet Walker, managing editor, The Preservation Press. Editorial assistance provided by Paul Wolman

Designed by Anne Masters, Washington, D.C.

Composed in Horley Old Style by Graftec Corporation, Washington, D.C.

Printed on 80-pound Mohawk Superfine by the John D. Lucas Printing Company, Baltimore, Md.

Cover: Postcard view of the bandstand (demolished) at East Lake Park, Los Angeles. (Smithsonian Institution, Hazen Collection)

CONTENTS

♪ ♪ ♪

FOREWORD

♪ ♪ ♪

There was a time, a century ago, when village bandstands on the green served as gathering places for communities all over America. Surviving bandstands with their whimsical gingerbread trim and the music of John Philip Sousa and Charles Ives still recall this phase of American cultural history. There is a need for a revival of such community vitality.

The small wooden bandstand that once stood on Tappan Square in Oberlin, Ohio, contributed to the town's community spirit by providing a stage for crowd-pleasing events ranging from concerts and plays to barber shop quartets and speeches. After the loss of the bandstand in 1907, this rhythm of

Oberlin's original bandstand on Tappan Square around 1900. (Oberlin College Archives)

community interaction largely disappeared, although Tappan Square continues to attract many leisure- and nature-lovers and is the setting for summer activities from May Day and commencement to the Fourth of July.

The architectural implications of a competition to design a new bandstand for Oberlin are nearly ideal in that there is no confusion as to history of type, specific meaning or precedent. A bandstand is as pure as architecture can be. The constraints are not complex, but are enriching and unencumbered. The design interpretations are infinite: an object—sculpture in a park—one that does not require plumbing, heating, air conditioning or closure, but must only be roofed and open sided, be four dimensional and accommodate a raised platform.

A bandstand is both symbolic and cultural. It simultaneously instills a sense of permanence and of speculation. It provokes memory and fantasy. It bridges the generations by seducing both the child, as a large-scale toy, and the adult, as a stage for dreams. It is the ultimate icon of freedom: freedom of choice, spirit and soul. It is about wonder and universality. Finally, it is a recognition of human ideals; there is no limit.

It is incredible that such a simple building can instill such presence and hope. This is what architectural competitions should also be about—not winning, but

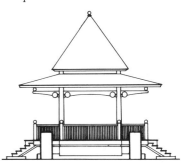

Clark Bandstand on Tappan Square in 1987. (Christopher Chalsma)

Detail of the winning drawing submitted by Julian S. Smith to The Great Bandstand Design Competition.

experiencing and contributing ideas through creative interpretation. Design competitions themselves, in seeking to realize an ideal, interpret ideas and needs through creative debate. Competitions are the most democratic process of design: the problem is posed, constraints such as site are imposed, and the designer is free to develop the building, drawing inspiration from history, philosophy or intuition.

Americans have a long tradition of using design competitions to interpret our collective ideals. Many of the most powerful symbols of our country were designed through competitions: the United States Capitol, the White House and many state capitol buildings. Monuments from the Washington Monument to the Vietnam Veterans Memorial in Wash-

ington, D.C., are a result of design competitions as are grand public spaces from Central Park in New York City to the Gateway Arch in St. Louis. In the end, a design competition, for a grand structure or a simple bandstand, generates a deeper understanding of a building or place by directly engaging the designers, reviewers and public in a search for excellence.

Everyone who participated in the Oberlin bandstand competition—the designers, the reviewers and the citizens of this small and vibrant Ohio town—has enriched our lives by giving us a rare moment of pure experience.

Charles Gwathmey, FAIA

ACKNOWLEDGMENTS

♪ ♪ ♪

A design competition and its documentation require the considerable help of a number of people. Oberlin College's competition to establish a new bandstand on Tappan Square in the heart of Oberlin, Ohio, has called on many. Among them, special acknowledgment goes to Grover E. Mouton III for his contributions to the development and organization of the competition and for his willing assistance in all phases of the process leading to publication of this volume.

The project would not have succeeded without financial assistance from the National Endowment for the Arts. Oberlin College is grateful for the challenge grants that led to the competition, the exhibition and this publication. Particular thanks go to Peter H. Smith of the Design Arts Program.

The editor extends special appreciation to Robert M. and Margaret Hindle Hazen for the use of their postcard collection, to Leona B. Holtz for sharing her bandstand photographs and to the many librarians and historians who responded generously to inquiries for information on bandstands in their towns.

The staff of the Allen Memorial Art Museum in Oberlin, and its able director, William J. Chiego, worked heroically to bring the bandstand competition project to fruition and to prepare The Great Bandstand Design Competition: Exhibition, May 2 to July 5, 1987. Mary Durling tenaciously nurtured both the competition and this book, while Barbara Chalsma,

director of communications at Oberlin College, provided editorial assistance.

Warm thanks also are due the committee and jury members listed below who helped make the new Oberlin bandstand a reality.

THE GREAT BANDSTAND DESIGN COMPETITION

Mary Durling, *Oberlin, Ohio, project director*
Theodore Liebman, FAIA, *New York City, professional adviser*
Grover E. Mouton III, *New Orleans, professional consultant*

OBERLIN COLLEGE ADVISORY COMMITTEE
Paul B. Arnold, *professor of art*
Jeremy Berkman, *class of 1986*
Geoffrey T. Blodgett, *professor of history, chairman*
Barbara Chalsma, *director of communications*
Christine Dyer, *former registrar, Allen Memorial Art Museum*
William E. Hood, *professor of art*
David A. Love, *associate provost*
S. Frederick Starr, *president*
M. Kirby Talley, Jr., *former director, Allen Memorial Art Museum*
Edward J. J. Thompson, *grounds manager*

JURY OF AWARD
Jack M. Bethards, *authority on American popular music of the period 1890–1950, San Francisco*
Geoffrey T. Blodgett, *professor of history, Oberlin College*
Ronald C. Filson, AIA, *dean, School of Architecture, Tulane University, New Orleans*
Ellen H. Johnson, *emerita professor of art, Oberlin College*
Roger G. Kennedy, *director, National Museum of American History, Smithsonian Institution, Washington, D. C.*
Laurie D. Olin, *chairman, Department of Landscape Architecture, Harvard Graduate School of Design, Cambridge, Mass.*
S. Frederick Starr, *jury chairman (nonvoting)*

AMERICAN BANDSTANDS

BANDSTANDS & AMERICAN URBANISM

S. FREDERICK STARR

In August 1895 Ada Minor of Champaign, Ill., received a postcard from her niece, Marion, vacationing in Waukesha, Wis. "This is a nice place," wrote Marion. "Band getting ready to play . . . it's swell here." The postcard, luridly colored, depicts the handsome bandstand at Bethesda Spring, near Waukesha.

Americans everywhere would have understood Marion's description of a summer idyll. To relax on the grass in a park, the local brass band seated on a picturesque bandstand and preparing to strike up an air—this was the quintessence of summer bliss in the United States for three generations. Most towns possessed a bandstand, and few failed to boast of the fact through the postcards available to visitors. From Fort Allen Park in Portland, Maine, to Wright Park in Tacoma, Wash., from City Park in Sheboygan, Wis., to Water Works Park in Atlanta, bandstands served as symbols of local identity, civic pride and a community's cultural commitment.

Today, bandstands evoke sentimental reveries of America's simpler days, of a time when innocence was still intact. Many small towns—places such as Togus, Maine; Milan, Ohio; and Ottumwa, Iowa—may once have fit this image. But in the post–Civil War era most American communities already were beset by powerful centrifugal forces. Industry and commerce had widened the gap between rich and poor. Successive waves of immigrants washed away homogeneity in religion and even language. Increasingly, the preacher, politician and writer spoke to and for his or her own. Tract housing isolated groups and classes as never before. Electric street railways enabled people to flee in whatever direction they wished, reinforcing their isolation.

Music has the power to bridge social and cultural barriers, however. The old town of Danbury, Conn., provides good testimony to this truth. The churches and political parties of the town were strictly segregated along ethnic lines by the 1880s. Yet the town band, led by cornetist George E. Ives (father of composer Charles Ives) embraced rich and poor, old Yankees, Irish and even a newly arrived Italian.[1]

To be sure, there were all manner of "tribal" bands made up exclusively of Sicilians or Germans, Catholics or Methodists, union members or scabs, blacks or whites. But the bandstand itself was everywhere considered neutral territory, and the audience assembled there was drawn from the entire community. Standing or sitting in an informal circle, members of the public faced one another in what was probably one of the few settings where Americans still smiled together. From the Civil War through World War I, bandstands were America's great social condensers, architectural embodiments of the national motto, *E pluribus unum*. Through them, the alienated individual was at least briefly reintegrated with society, which no doubt explains why so many mental institutions, from Jackson, La., to Jacksonville, Ill., had bandstands at their center.

Thousands of bandstands were erected in America's towns and cities. Only a few remain today. From old postcards and town records, however, one quickly discovers the stunning diversity of their architecture and of their role in the urban fabric. Anyone seeking to build a bandstand today can draw on an inexhaustible wealth of historic models.

THE PROTOTYPE

Few bandstands were built before the Civil War. The manufacture of piston-valved horns was still in its infancy, and the meeting house, town hall and church still met Americans' need for assembly space. True, even small towns such as Oberlin, Ohio, had brass bands by the outbreak of the Civil War. But few bandstands were erected until after Appomattox. It is very likely that weary veterans, both Blue and Gray,

Drawing of a bandstand by Richard Morris Hunt, submitted to a Parisian competition in 1849. Here the bandstand is more nearly a theatrical stage. (Prints and Drawings Collection, Octagon Museum, Washington, D.C.)

promoted local band concerts as a nostalgic evocation of wartime camp life, recalled in the peaceful setting of family and community.

We know that one of the first American architects to design a bandstand was Richard Morris Hunt, who did so as a student in Paris in 1849.[2] With its Italianate formalism and stage-set plan, Hunt's proposal was better suited to the Bois du Boulogne than to an American town square. Designs that gained popularity in America were far simpler. Typical is one built in 1905 and still standing in the park in Traer, Iowa. Hexagonal in plan, this plain but expressive structure could have been built in a few days by amateur carpenters. The same simplicity is achieved in the bandstands in Reading, Pa.; in the town of Central Square, N.Y.; and in City Park in Houston, Tex. This simple boothlike prototype was repeated for years; the bandstand in Lunenburg, Mass., in 1905 was nearly identical to those built in

Bandstand (1905; rehabilitated, 1977), Traer, Iowa. (Hazen Collection)

Bandstand (c. 1905–10; rebuilt 1960), City Park, Houston. (Hazen Collection)

the 1870s.[3] Nearly all such basic stands were hexagonal, octagonal or circular in plan. Only a handful, such as those in Central Park in Newark, N.Y.; City Park in Topeka, Kans.; or on Lake Quassapaug, Conn., were square. Bandstands with square plans had the disadvantage of urging the audience into only one quadrant of the surrounding area, thus reducing informality and sociability.

Some of these prototypical stands were exceptionally simple—the ones in Oberlin, Ohio, or Sterling, Kans., for example. Builders wishing more could either dress up the roofline with machine-made brackets and store-bought "gingerbread" or give the roof a steeper pitch. In Madrid, N.Y., and Baldwinville, Mass., both methods were applied with great effectiveness.

From the outset, bandstands served multiple functions. The one in Leighton, Pa., was intended as much as a reviewing stand for parades as to mount concerts. The tiny "bandstand" in Norwich, N.Y., was probably also used for reviewing parades, if not for selling lemonade, but was much too small to house a full ensemble of musicians. Whatever their function, the simplest stands were sited almost casually, whether along a main street, on a central square or, as in Exeter, N.H., in the middle of an intersection. They were not, in short, viewed as important elements in the landscape plan.

Thanks to their simplicity, these basic stands were inexpensive. The one in Newark, N.Y., cost only $800 in 1906,[4] whereas a similar stand in McClure Park in Newton, Ind., cost only $982.75 in 1924.[5] Even

Concrete block bandstand (1906), Newark, N.Y., saved after a successful campaign by preservationists. (Hazen Collection)

Bandstand (1905), Lunenburg, Mass. Concerts here were lighted by electricity from the nearby trolley line. Lights dimmed whenever a trolley passed, however. (Hazen Collection)

Frederick Law Olmsted and Calvert Vaux's 1872 construction budget for Central Park in New York City included only $5,000 out of $1,500,000 for "music platforms, arbors and seats."[6]

Who paid for these prototypical bandstands? In Traer, Iowa, the city council levied a tax to cover the expense.[7] Local tradition in Ligonier, Pa., holds that the zealous members of the town's cornet band raised the money themselves.[8] The handsome bandstand at the steamboat landing in Kingston, N.Y., was built by local concessionaires; while the one at the popular Spanish Fort amusement park near New Orleans was constructed by the private proprietors of that establishment. Sometimes even individual families built bandstands, for example, the Frantzis family, which

Original bandstand (1879; burned, 1907) on Tappan Square, Oberlin, Ohio. (Oberlin College Archives)

ran the popular resort on Lake Quassapaug, Conn. Increasingly, however, as bandstands came to be seen as necessary fixtures of public parks, they were paid for by municipal governments.

NATURE AND THE BANDSTAND

Initially, bandstands were conceived purely as functional pieces of civic architecture, a no-nonsense view that lived on in many small cities and towns. Bandstands were placed at whatever point in-town convenience might dictate. If planning considerations entered at all, they led to the placement of bandstands on some main axis in the public square. A fresh current in landscape architecture, however, caused Americans increasingly to view bandstands and similar structures as vital links between people and Nature. The new sensibility dictated that the bandstand fit picturesquely

Rectangular bandstand (c. 1908) on Lake Quassapaug, Middlebury, Conn., demolished for being unsafe in the 1960s. (Hazen Collection)

From Calvert Vaux's 1857 volume, Villas and Cottages, *three garden houses foreshadowing the rustic approach to bandstand design. (Dover Publications)*

into a pastoral landscape, like a peasant bower in a painting by Claude Lorrain.[9]

The bucolic conception of the bandstand had been set forth before the Civil War by landscape architect Andrew Jackson Downing in *A Treatise on the Theory and Practice of Landscape Gardening*. "There is scarcely a prettier or more pleasant object for the termination of a long walk in the pleasure grounds or park," Downing declared, "than a neatly thatched structure of rustic work."[10] The gazebos he contrived to fill this function were in fact prototypes for a new form of bandstand.

It remained for Frederick Law Olmsted, architect of New York City's Central Park, to draw the link between such sylvan bowers and music. "The effect of good music on the Park," he wrote, "is to aid the mind in freeing itself from the irritating effect of the urban conditions . . . ."[11] In other words, the modern city

should contain its own antidote in the form of rural parks, which should be sprinkled with garden houses, gazebos, pavilions and "concert groves," where weary urbanites would be soothed by dulcet tunes.

Whether under the influence of such theoretical statements or on their own impulses, Americans of the late 19th century were concluding that rustic parks and band music were needed to humanize the industrial city. The resulting bandstands were designed to serve as settings for informal concerts and, at other times, as belvederes from which strollers could view their pleasant surroundings. To enhance their function as belvederes, bandstands were elevated further from the ground. The one on King's Square in Whitefield, N.H., was raised half a floor above the surrounding grass, as were the bandstands in City Park in Sheboygan, Wis., and Goshen, Ind. A local historian in Traer, Iowa, reports that the bandstand there was so high that it was rarely, if ever, used for musical performances.[12]

Under the influence of the Picturesque movement, the distinction between bandstands and belvederes vanished. It is doubtful that the diminutive turn-of-the-century bandstand in City Park, Oconomowoc, Wis., hosted many band concerts, but it provided a lovely view of the nearby lake, as did the contemporary gazebo-bandstand in Cincinnati's Eden Park.

Many of the nation's most gracefully sited stands and gazebos are adjacent to water. Bandstand pavilions in Portland, Maine; Wakefield, Mass.; Riverside, N.J.;

Pueblo, Colo.; and Ontario Beach, N.Y., are architecturally diverse but functionally similar—all are prospect points for viewing soothing coastal or riverside scenes.

Many bandstands were built near piers for the holiday steamers that were so popular in 19th-century America. In Sag Harbor, Long Island, N.Y., for example, and New London, Conn., bandstands were situated to enable bands to serenade arriving and departing tourists. In Narragansett and Providence, R.I., similarly placed bandstands served as visual links

Bandstand (c. 1915) in City Park, Oconomowoc, Wis., replaced by a band shell in the 1930s by the WPA. (Hazen Collection)

between the piers and adjacent casinos. Intended to serve revelers, these bandstands functioned equally as belvederes from which urban Americans could survey a carefully tamed Nature.

BANDSTANDS AS URBAN SCULPTURE

In his early planning for Central Park, Frederick Law Olmsted cautioned against "grandiose [architectural] display" that would distract from one's appreciation of nature. By 1880, however, Olmsted's restraint was out of fashion. Even his former partner, Calvert Vaux, was conjuring up more elaborate bandstands, and in city after city architects and builders competed to achieve ever-more extravagant displays of virtuosity. More modest bandstands continued to be built, but they were no longer the rule. The availability of inexpensive mill work and factory-made turnings, such as columns and balustrades, as well as polychrome tiles and cast-iron columns and handrails, was an irresistible temptation both to big-city promoters and to small-town boosters. Bandstands thus took on yet another function—to serve as bright and whimsical pieces of urban sculpture.

For some builders, the urge toward greater expressiveness was satisfied by the use of innovative plans. The pagoda of 1878–79 in Jacksonville, Ill. (now at the Smithsonian Institution in Washington, D.C.) is a miniaturized rustic villa without walls, its complex roof structure paralleling the unusual linear plan. Monticello, Ind., boasts a bandstand of similar linear plan, although not as complex.

Top: Lithographic view of Central Park, New York City, in 1861. (J. Clarence Davies Collection, Museum of the City of New York)

Above: Summer house (c. 1860; rebuilt 1985) in Central Park overlooking 59th Street. (Museum of the City of New York)

Sheet music cover published in 1863 by the famous cornetist and bandleader H. B. Dodworth. The floating music pavilion depicted here was the central feature of New York City's Central Park. (Museum of the City of New York)

Others met the demand for greater expressiveness through daring siting, usually involving water. As early as 1863 a "floating bandstand" was being promoted on sheet music celebrating New York City's Central Park.[13] The same idea was realized in Jersey City, N.J., with a bandstand built on piers over a lake and connected to land by a footbridge. For Onondaga Park in Syracuse, N.Y., a circular bandstand was constructed on an artificial island. At both Union Park in Des Moines and Belle Isle in Detroit, bandstands were erected over the water. The latter was a square structure built on a bridge spanning a lagoon.

The most ambitious effort in this direction was made in 1878 at Forest Park in St. Louis. A large and intricate folly by local architect James Stewart dominated the artificial island. Nominally of "Syrian" design but known locally as the music pagoda, Stewart's polychrome monument featured a bulbous dome over a wild collection of Moorish porticoes.[14] Stewart's was not the only bandstand built in the Moorish style. Another fine one from 1900 still stands at the Veterans Home in Yountville, Calif.[15] But Stewart's creation was by far the most flamboyant. Doubtless, he felt compelled to outdo St. Louis's Tower Grove Park bandstand, built five years before by another local architect, Eugene L. Greenleaf. Stewart succeeded grandly, although the Tower Grove Park structure has outlived his pagoda.

The St. Louis bandstands attest to a basic characteristic of the form: the requirement that the sides be fully open to the audience forces the designers to concentrate their inventiveness on the roof. Thus,

Music pagoda (1876) in Forest Park, St. Louis. This bandstand broke new ground for flamboyance and eclecticism. Declared unsafe in 1911, it succumbed to a storm in 1912. (Missouri Botanical Garden Library, St. Louis)

when civic leaders in Bellville, Ohio, engaged Abraham Lash in 1879 to design a bandstand, he proposed a simple octagonal structure but capped it with a gloriously elaborate gingerbread canopy.

Heavy closed domes of various forms were not uncommon, whether on a modest scale as in Ligonier, Pa., or as seen in more grandiose variants such as in Waukesha, Wis. Some genuinely original solutions emerged. In Bath, N.Y., an unknown architect raised

Left: Bandstand (1878–79) at the Illinois Central Hospital for the Insane, Jacksonville, Ill., in 1905. The structure now is located on the National Mall, Washington, D.C. (Smithsonian Institution)

"Music stand" (1872) in Tower Grove Park, St. Louis, designed by Eugene L. Greenleaf to rest on an artificial elevation. (Hazen Collection)

a clerestory above a square bandstand, topping it in turn with a pagoda-like roof. At Island Park in Tilton, N.H., a breathtaking display of folkish fretwork leads to three levels of roofs with a soaring carved heron spreading its wings over the entire structure. Even if inspiration failed, one could always borrow from others. The builder of the bandstand in Kingston Point, N.Y., met his need for a lively roof design by taking over a pattern normally used for merry-go-rounds.

Amidst such a welter of fantasy it was inevitable that primitivist urges would make themselves felt. There is evidence that Abraham Lash in Bellville was inspired by rustic garden gazebos, which he knew from his days as a florist in fashionable Cleveland suburbs.[16] More deliberately rustic is the Forest Park bandstand in Little Rock, Ark., where a traditional octagonal structure is constructed in the rough-hewn manner of Adirondack mountain lodges. Olmsted had used the same concept in Central Park, but only for garden houses and gazebos. More aggressively primitive is the roofless bandstand in Wright Park in Tacoma, Wash. Here rough-hewn timbers are bunched to look like the trunk of a single vast spruce tree, typical of the Pacific Northwest. By contrast, the "indigenous" style of the band pavilion in Watertown,

Top: Summer house (after 1865; destroyed by hurricane), Island Park, Tilton, N.H., once one of the most fanciful and original bandstands in the country. (Library of Congress)

Right: Bandstand (1879) in Bellville, Ohio, a gingerbread classic by Abraham Lash and still the object of pilgrimages to his hometown. (Mary Durling, 1987)

Right: Bandstand (1903; demolished), Forest Park, Little Rock, Ark., a rustic octagon built by the local streetcar company. (Hazen Collection)

Below: Pavilion (1894), Ligonier, Pa., built with funds raised by the local cornet band. (Leona B. Holtz, 1984)

Below: Bandstand (1893; demolished) in Kingston, N.Y., on the Hudson River, built so that brass bands could greet tourists arriving from New York City. (Hazen Collection, Edwin M. Ford)

Above: Tree-stump bandstand (before 1922; demolished), Wright Park, Tacoma, Wash. (Hazen Collection)

Wis., is almost neoclassical in its elegance, notwithstanding its obvious reference to the local Prairie School style of Frank Lloyd Wright.

BANDSTANDS FOR THE CITY BEAUTIFUL

The quest for sculptural exotica threatened to tear the concept of a bandstand from its functional moorings in music and landscape architecture. But before the drive for ever-more exotic bandstands had peaked after 1900, new developments in both town planning and music caused the designers of bandstands to rethink the function, design and location of their structures. The City Beautiful movement set bandstand design on a fresh course.

Whereas the urban park movement's goal was to establish islands of bucolic beauty amidst ugly and inhospitable cities, the City Beautiful movement's objective was to turn the entire metropolis into a work of art. The new movement took inspiration from Baron Hausmann's Paris and gained practical backing from the industrial wealth and local pride that flowed into some 1,200 civic improvement societies across the country. Participants in this movement share a body of ideas learned from personal experience and drawn from the climate of the times. Charles Mulford Robinson's *The Improvement of Towns and Cities, or The Practical Basis of Civic Aesthetics* (1901) and his *Modern Civic Art, or The City Made Beautiful* (2d ed., 1903) only codified what right-thinking civic leaders already believed—namely, that a "world-wide civic battle" was being waged "between Ugliness and Beauty."[17] The task of the City Beautiful movement was to impose firm principles of beauty on the disorderly growth of urban America.

This impetus found expression in a growing formality and complexity of park design. Where formerly curvilinear paths had prevailed, now there were axial promenades; where there were rustic gazebos and leafy bowers, now there were Roman or Renaissance-style pavilions and rigid rows of trimmed trees interspersed with urns and fountains. Returning to Richard Morris Hunt's point of departure of a half century earlier, bandstand designers now embraced the baroque gardens that Downing and Olmsted had spurned.

From New York City's Central Park to San Francisco's Golden Gate Park the new ideal became ubiquitous. The new bandstands were expensive, unlike their predecessors. An up-to-date "temple of music" (as the bandstand in Golden Gate Park was called) could cost as much as $75,000.[18] There was nothing temporary about these monuments: the colonnaded Renaissance edifice in San Francisco was built entirely of Colusa sandstone. Even modest-sized bandstands of the new type, such as that in City Park in Ottumwa, Iowa, have an air of permanence thanks to their imposing locations at the junction of strict axial paths.

The growing importance of large, professional bands reinforced the new trend in bandstand design, especially after World War I. National touring ensembles under the batons of such luminaries as John Philip Sousa and Arthur Pryor could steal the

Top: San Francisco's bandstand (1900) in Golden Gate Park, designed as a "temple of music." (Hazen Collection)

Above: Pavilion and bandstand (c. 1880; demolished) in New Orleans's West End in 1901. The bandstand handled the larger ensembles popular in the 1900s. (Library of Congress)

show wherever they appeared. These big spit-and-polish bands required far larger pavilions than the traditional, small local groups, and their eminence caused audiences to want to sit attentively in rows of seats rather than loll about on the grass. This, plus the demand for better acoustics that the national bands inspired, led gradually to the decline of the old three-dimensional bandstands and the rise of monodirectional band shells.

At Luna Park in Hartford, Conn., for example, a typical three-dimensional exotic bandstand looked out not on a grassy field but on rows of hard-backed seats. And by 1901 the proprietors of West End, near New Orleans, closed in the back side of their traditional octagonal gazebo to project the sound forward; they then extended the front to provide a rectangular space in front of the neat rows of seats.[19]

The new sensibility inspired some magnificent structures. By 1912 Olmsted's South Park in Rochester, N.Y., boasted a large acoustical band shell flanked by high brick and masonry piers with a balustrade across its front. The builders of Carnival Park in Kansas City, Kans., chose a vast neoclassical arch, closed at the back to form a proscenium stage. The new band shell at Central Park in New York City brought together Roman motifs in a large masonry structure worthy of a Renaissance palace garden.

Amidst all the lavishness of design and construction were a few original conceptions. The band shell built at Michigan State College (now University) in East Lansing presents a curvilinear facade reminiscent of works by the Belgian Art Nouveau architect Henri

Band shell (c. 1912; demolished), South Park, Rochester, N.Y. Here planners rejected the classic three-dimensional form and embraced the fashionable band shell, losing a sense of informality but gaining better acoustics. (Hazen Collection)

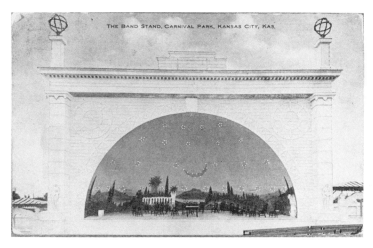

THE BAND STAND, CARNIVAL PARK, KANSAS CITY, KAS.

Top: Proscenium-type band shell (1907–11; dismantled) in Carnival Park, Kansas City, Kans. The backdrop anticipated the exotic interiors of movie palaces of the 1920s. (Hazen Collection)

Above: Band shell (c. 1907) in Pioneer Park, Lewiston, Idaho, a one-of-a-kind shell replaced in 1956 by a concrete utility building. (Nez Perce Historical Society, Inc.)

van der Velde. More interesting still was the band shell at Pioneer Park in Lewiston, Idaho. Built before 1907, this modest hemispherical wooden structure is the epitome of functionalism. Its only ornament is a crest on the top, which makes the shell resemble a Prussian helmet. Like so many of the best American bandstands, however, this one had fallen to the wrecker's ball by 1936.

CODA AND FINALE: 1920–40

By World War I the entire range of urban ideals that had inspired the construction of thousands of bandstands nationwide was under attack from every side. Henry Ford's Model Ts now enabled Americans to motor through the countryside on Saturday afternoon rather than congregate with neighbors around the bandstand. Vernon and Irene Castle had set the whole country dancing the one-step, two-step, shimmy and fox trot. Shorter hemlines, bobbed hair, soft collars and the pocket flask reflected young Americans' determined assault on their parents' Victorian mores. Jazz, which crystallized these developments, lured musicians and audiences alike. Recordings—Sousa denounced them as "canned music"—and the radio made national bands accessible to everyone. The old-time local band concert now seemed hopelessly tame.

Old bandstands fell into disuse. Construction of many new ones was postponed or canceled. Automobile manufacturer William Dowd Packard of Warren, Ohio, endowed a bandstand for his hometown in

1920, but it was never built. Instead, his bequest was diverted to build a large civic auditorium in the 1950s. In Chesterton, Ind., a new bandstand was dedicated in 1924, but only after its backers had fought off several efforts to turn the downtown park in which it was situated into a parking lot. [20]

Nonetheless, bandstands continued to be built in some numbers until World War II. At McCulloch Park in Fort Wayne and at Fort Benjamin Harrison, both in Indiana, charmingly simple bandstands were constructed in 1930 and 1939, respectively, the former with money from the nearby General Electric factory.[22] Nor were all new bandstands simply repetitions of older prototypes. An example of continuing innovation is the bizarre but successful rectilinear bandstand constructed into the side of a hipped-roof barn in Mexico, N.Y., during these years.

Franklin Roosevelt's Work Projects Administration (WPA) was responsible for the penultimate burst of bandstand construction. At Mesilla Plaza in Old Mesilla, N.M., and at Old Town Plaza in Albuquerque, the WPA erected simple but effective bandstands in 1936. Neither, however, owed its existence to local initiative, and both became the object of controversy because their traditional design had nothing in common with the surrounding indigenous architecture of the old Southwest.[23] The lack of initiative in these cases is scarcely surprising, for by now both the brass-band movement and the instinct for urban sociability that underlay it were moribund in most American cities and towns.

DA CAPO

The story is not over. During the past two generations Americans have had ample reason to reflect seriously on the quality of urban life. In the 1950s suburbanization, ghettoization, "white flight" and the decay of core cities became the verbal emblems of our urban pathology. In a vain attempt to improve the situation, rotting structures were swept away, while whole districts were planned and constructed *de novo*. Too often the graduates of newly created academic programs in urban planning arrogantly replaced the old with faceless schemes whose only virtue—and not a lasting one—was their newness.

With the publication of Jane Jacobs's *The Death and Life of Great American Cities* in 1961, a more positive mood began to set in as Americans looked with fresh eyes at what they had been so blithely destroying under the banner of "renewal." In dozens of towns and cities this led to the restoration of crumbling bandstands, and even to the erection of totally new structures for civic music designed in the old spirit. Not since the decade 1900–10 have so many bandstands been constructed in the United States, nor have they seen such intensive use since before the era of "canned music" and televised sociability.

Oberlin, Ohio, is by no means the first community to seek to recapture some of the human values formerly epitomized by the town bandstand and the Saturday afternoon concert. But Oberlin does have a distinctive relation to America's much-debated small-town values, and this makes Oberlin's new Clark Bandstand of special interest. Sinclair Lewis, who

Bandstand (1936), Old Mesilla, N.M., a stripped-down bandstand design supported by the WPA. (L. O. Candelaria, Candelaria Color Graphics)

Bandstand (1936) on Old Town Plaza, Albuquerque, a source of controversy when it was built because it was not in the then-popular Spanish style. (L. O. Candelaria, Candelaria Color Graphics)

criticized provincial life in such novels as *Main Street* and *Babbitt,* studied at Oberlin College, as did playwright Thornton Wilder, author of *Our Town* and one of the fondest admirers of the village community in America. Sherwood Anderson, author of *Winesburg, Ohio,* also grew up nearby; he, too, was preoccupied with the tension between local and cosmopolitan values. Oberlin has a town band dating to the 1850s, and its older residents treasure memories of concerts at the local bandstand, long since demolished. No wonder, then, that this was the ideal town to try to put into action the old notion of strengthening neighborly bonds through civic gatherings around a bandstand. If Oberlin's success to date is any indication of the situation nationally, one can conclude that the old roots are still alive and capable of sending forth new shoots. ♪ ♪ ♪

NOTES

1. Frank R. Rossiter, *Charles Ives and His America* (New York: Liveright, 1975), p. 37.

2. Susan R. Stein, ed., *The Architecture of Richard Morris Hunt* (Chicago: University of Chicago Press, 1986), pp. 28–29.

3. Nelde K. Drumm and Margaret P. Harley, *Lunenburg: The Heritage of Turkey Hills, 1718–1978* (Lunenburg, Mass.: Lunenburg Historical Society, 1977), p. 302 ff. Courtesy of Helen Brown, Lunenburg, Mass.

4. Village Board Minutes, Newark, N.Y., July 20, 1906. Courtesy of Mrs. Herbert Jackson, Newark, N.Y.

5. "The Bandstand," *Selmer Bandwagon,* No. 92, 1980, p. 12.

6. F. L. Olmsted, Jr., and Theodora Kimball, eds., *Frederick Law Olmsted: Landscape Architect, 1822–1903* (New York: Benjamin Blom, 1970), p. 292.

7. Minutes of City Council, Traer, Iowa, 1901. Courtesy of Dale Ross, Buckingham, Iowa.

8. Reported by Sherry Massimo, Ligonier Valley Library, Ligonier, Pa., 1987.

9. Elizabeth Barlow, *Frederick Law Olmsted's New York* (New York: Praeger, 1972), p. 10 ff.

10. Andrew Jackson Downing, *A Treatise on the Theory and Practice of Landscape Gardening* (New York: C. M. Saxton, 1855), p. 456.

11. F. L. Olmsted, Jr., and Theordora Kimball, *Frederick Law Olmsted: Landscape Architect,* p. 252.

12. Personal correspondence between Dale Ross, Buckingham, Iowa, and Mary Durling, Oberlin, Ohio, 1987.

13. Bruce Kelly et al., *Art of the Olmsted Landscape* (New York: New York City Landmarks Preservation Commission, 1981), plates 54–55.

14. City of St. Louis, Department of Parks, Recreation and Forestry, *Inventory of Structures* (St. Louis: Author, n.d.), unnumbered pages.

15. Courtesy of Jack L. Siemers, Yountville, Calif., 1987.

16. *Richland Star* (Bellville, Ohio), September 11, 1879. Courtesy of Martha Palm, Bellville, Ohio.

17. C. M. Robinson, *The Improvement of Towns and Cities* (New York: G. P. Putnam's Sons, 1901), p. 294.

18. Courtesy of the Public Information Office, San Francisco Recreation and Parks Department, 1987.

19. Leonard V. Huber, *New Orleans: A Pictorial History* (New York: Bonanza Books, 1980), p. 231.

20. *Lewiston Morning Tribune,* March 30, 1956. Courtesy of Nez Perce Historical Society, Lewiston, Idaho.

21. *Selmer Bandwagon,* No. 92, p. 11.

22. *Ibid,* p. 12.

23. Courtesy of Jill Baxter, Reference Section, Albuquerque Public Library, and Sue Richmond, Las Cruces Library, 1987.

THE BAND MOVEMENT

MARGARET HINDLE HAZEN

"The band is now king!" With these enthusiastic words the editor of a popular music journal inaugurated the summer band season of 1899. It was a dramatic but essentially true statement, for bands were the most popular musical organizations of the day. They performed virtually everywhere—at picnics and parties, dances and rallies, weddings and funerals. Almost any public occasion could be enhanced by band music, and some events, such as patriotic celebrations and circus performances, were unthinkable without it. By the end of the 19th century, open-air concerts in the community bandstand had become so integrated into American life that people often arranged their weekly routines around performances.

Enthusiasm for bands seemed to transcend the racial, ethnic, regional and class divisions of turn-of-the-century America. Blacks and Native Americans played in bands, as did men, and occasionally women, from every ethnic group in the country. Rustic communities in the Far West nurtured bands with the same fervor as did established New England townships, and one Rocky Mountain settlement is known to have had a band even before the town had a proper name. Although many community bands attracted young men in their 20s and 30s, no age group was immune from band fever. Photographs reveal players as young as eight and as old as 80. Drafting toddlers as mascots and octogenarians as drum majors, some bands encompassed four generations.

Because of the sporadic existence of many bands, statistics on the size of the movement are elusive. A 1908 observer placed the number of bands in America at about 20,000. A prestigious musical periodical in the same year put the figure at more than 46,000. In either case, it is clear that hundreds of thousands of musicians were actively engaged in band work when the movement reached its peak just before World War I. Because so many players had drifted in and out of the band world over the previous decades and because many more citizens had supported the art form during that time, it is also clear that the band movement as a whole must have encompassed millions. Thus, it was one of the the most widespread and all-embracing cultural movements to appear in pre–World War II America.

THE BRASS BAND

What explains this phenomenon? In a country that bred more than its share of no-nonsense individuals professing to prefer the sound of singing telegraph wires and humming dynamos to any sort of music, the blossoming of America's brass bands, along with their fanciful bandstands, may seem a small miracle. But if it was a miracle, it was ironically one of practical invention, for it was in the first half of the

19th century that instrument makers perfected innovations in metal-working technology that enabled brass instruments to play chromatic and diatonic scales and, hence, melodies. The technical innovations transformed the shape, sound and dimensions of band music.

In the days of Mozart and Haydn, bands were predominantly woodwind ensembles that relied on oboes and clarinets to carry the melodies. Early wind bands typically were composed of pairs of oboes, clarinets, horns and bassoons. Trumpets, if used at all, were primarily for rhythmic emphasis. This balance changed decisively during the early 19th century as the new chromatic brass instruments were introduced. The keyed bugle, patented in 1810 by the Irish maker Joseph Haliday, made its appearance in the United States as early as 1815. The instrument was essentially a bugle equipped with saxophone-like keys to effect pitch changes. Soon, other novel chromatic brass instruments appeared,

Band concert (c. 1917), Hampton Beach, N.H. The bandstand (c. 1902) was replaced by a band shell in 1963. (Lake County Museum, Curt Teich Postcard Collection)

including the ophicleide (a larger and lower-pitched relative of the keyed bugle) and a whole variety of valved instruments. Adolphe Sax, inventor of the saxophone, produced entire families of matched valved instruments in Paris, as did instrument makers in the United States, so that by 1850, reliable chromatic brass instruments were available in every tonal register. Now brass instruments could be used not only for melodies but for every harmonic line as well.

Public response to these developments was phenomenal. Concurrent improvements in transportation meant that the tantalizing new instruments, along with skilled craftsmen who could make them and trained musicians who could teach them, were more easily conveyed to American shores and across the continent. Once introduced, these instruments proved especially suitable for mass music making. Not only were they loud and durable and thus unequaled for outdoor performances, they also could—in small groups or large—render any music, playing

Kingston Cornet Band of Kingston, N.H. (c. 1885), lashed together on a pair of boats to form a floating bandstand. Brass music travels clearly and far over water, so the ensemble could entertain a large crowd. (Kingston, N.H., Historical Society)

from the simplest patriotic song to the grandest operatic excerpt. Furthermore, although playing the keyed bugle and ophicleide required considerable expertise, this was not so of the valved brass instruments that superseded them. And because entire families of valved brass such as "saxhorns" used similar fingering systems and mouthpieces, members of a brass band could learn how to play at the same time and could even exchange instruments according to the needs of the group. Suddenly, bands did not require an elite corps of highly skilled musicians but could be composed of interested amateurs. A better musical medium for a democratic society hardly could have existed. The widespread formation of brass bands became almost inevitable.

Initially, the new brass instruments were integrated into traditional wind bands to enrich and strengthen the sound. But as early as the 1830s, professional and amateur groups began to switch to all-brass instrumentation. "The band has thrown aside all the wooden instruments formerly used by them and supplied their place with brass ones," enthused a New York City newspaper report. Hundreds of communities and organizations that had never sponsored bands quickly joined in the excitement and launched their own all-brass bands during the 1840s and 1850s.

By mid-century the trend to all-brass bands was so decisive that Boston music critic John Sullivan Dwight worried that wooden instruments might disappear altogether. Of course, this did not happen, but brass bands clearly had become the preferred format for public music making. Their effectiveness as military adjuncts was demonstrated repeatedly at militia exercises and was underscored dramatically during the Civil War, when tens of thousands of band players enlisted and offered musical inspiration and solace to their fellow soldiers.

But it was in peacetime—in the rousing, expansionist decades of the late 19th century—that the genre flowered as never before. Professional players led the way. Talented soloists such as Matthew Arbuckle, Jules Levy and Alessandro Liberati devoted their lives to band music and demonstrated the remarkable capabilities of the band's premier instrument, the cornet. They were supported by a battery of first-rate professional ensembles. The most famous were led by Patrick Gilmore and John Philip Sousa. Whether crisscrossing the country on extensive tours or appearing as featured entertainers at big-city amusement parks, these groups, along with the many other superb professional organizations that sprang up in their wake, ably demonstrated to admiring crowds the marvelous musical effects that could be achieved by large and well-drilled bands. Although most professional bandleaders had long since reintroduced woodwinds to balance the brass, there was no doubt that these musicians were perpetuating the spirit of the traditional brass band.

Inspired by the professionals, amateurs by the hundreds of thousands took up the art form. Factory workers, miners, railroad employees and cowboys played in bands sponsored by employers or labor unions. Members of men's clubs joined bands. So did newspaper carriers, orphans and schoolchildren. In response to the widespread late 19th-century belief in the rehabilitative and healthful effects of music, penitentiaries, hospitals and even a Hawaiian leper colony promoted band activities for their inmates. Apart from these influences, amateur players were strongly encouraged by American instrument manufacturers, who not only produced a wide range of inexpensive band instruments but also supplied nearly everything else an aspiring band might need to get started, including music, instruction manuals and even inspiration. "Anybody, with but few exceptions, if he likes music, can learn to play," promised a Wurlitzer Company advertisement. And, indeed, almost everybody seems to have taken up the challenge.

By far the most common and cherished of the avocational bands were the town bands organized throughout the country by music-loving citizens. At

Davenport, Iowa, Silver Band (c. 1870), posing for stereographer L. N. Cook. The Odd Fellows' "chariot" float is just behind. The band played a set of overshoulder brass instruments, ideal for leading a parade and setting the tempo. (Hazen Collection)

the turn of the 20th century some villages with only a few hundred inhabitants could boast a band of 10 or 12 pieces, and many modest-sized communities supported several such performing groups. Most band players joined without any appreciable musical knowledge, but they paid dues, drafted detailed bylaws, purchased instruments and usually attended rehearsals dutifully. That they sometimes received a pittance for their performances in no way alters the fact that they devoted substantial amounts of time, energy and personal income to their hobby.

THE ARDENT PUBLIC

The American public seems to have been as enthusiastic about bands as were the players. They bought tickets to dime concerts as readily as they bought dime novels.

They congregated, sometimes in excessive heat and cold, to hear the bands play. Generous band boosters did even more. Through fund-raising events, donations and even municipal taxes they helped their bands purchase shiny new instruments and elegant uniforms. And once the musicians had mastered their art—frequently using the local school or town hall for rehearsals—the most devoted listeners constructed pavilions in which the bands could play.

And why not? The return on their investment could hardly have been more satisfying. Most bands were willing to play whenever and wherever the public desired. They seemed equally at home on land, in boats or in diminutive bandstands in the middle of lakes. Versatile band musicians could play while marching in a parade or at a promenade concert, where they would sit while a fashionable audience marched past. As for the music, it was virtually guaranteed to please. Artfully combining lightweight patriotic tunes and romantic songs with more substantial virtuoso showpieces and classical transcriptions, the average band concert program was designed to appeal to the tastes of all.

Bands also had a lofty social purpose. As newspaper editors, music journalists and instrument company representatives frequently explained, bands were only slightly less important to the advancement of civilization than the pulpit and press, railroads or—as one expert saw it toward the end of the gritty 19th century—fresh air and pure water. Accordingly, 19th-century publications are full of anecdotes that feature brass bands as agents of cultural uplift. One typical story features a midwestern town in which, to an eastern visitor's horror, a hotel is run by a bored-looking innkeeper who does nothing more than stare all day at the swine in his yard.

"Don't you get tired of looking at hogs and pigs?" the visitor asks the sleepy innkeeper.

"Reckon not," answers the latter. "Hain't got nothin' else to look at, an' their squealin' kind o' keeps a feller company.

"See here, my friend," says the visitor warmly, "you people need civilizing. What you want in this vicinity is a good live brass band. That will wake you up.

"Maybe 'twould, mister," answers the native. "Just bring it on an' we'll see!"

As the story goes, the visitor did so with the happy result that, one year later, no more hogs were running loose in town and the indifferent looks had vanished entirely from the innkeeper's face.

The composer Charles Ives, son of a bandmaster, was intimately acquainted with bands and the mystique that surrounded them. In tribute, he incorporated the blaring sounds of brass bands in his orchestral composition *Holidays*. Written between 1904 and 1913, the piece successfully captures the vibrant spirit of the band movement when it was in its glory.

THE WANING YEARS

In a sense, Ives's innovative composition was written just in time. Within a few short years, the public's

Mineral City, Ohio, Cornet Band, a typical 12-piece small-town brass band of the 1890s. Ten brass instruments ranging from E-flat cornet to E-flat tuba, plus bass drum and side drum, were a standard mixture. (Hazen Collection)

enthusiasm for bands had begun to wane, and the number of performing groups commenced a slow but steady decline. In some localities amateur bands yielded to the emerging school bands in town. In others, the removal of a centrally located bandstand to ease downtown traffic congestion started a cycle of organizational problems from which the band could not recover. In still others, musicians—as well as their audiences—found other ways to use and enjoy their leisure and simply allowed the bands to fold. The rise of radio broadcasting was of paramount importance in this regard, but the appearance of automobiles, phonographs and motion pictures was also significant. Not only did these new pastimes lure audiences and musicians away from band performances, but in permitting—even promoting—the segregation of leisured Americans according to variables of age, cultural taste and income, these new activities also severely undercut the communal solidarity that had always been so fundamental to the band movement. Furthermore, in carrying the high-quality and increasingly jazzy sounds of professional bands to more people than ever before, the radio and the phonograph indirectly provoked negative feelings about amateur local talent and their presentations of what was rapidly becoming old-fashioned music. Faced with indifference or even hostility on the part of increasingly sophisticated audiences, many amateur and traditional professional bands languished and lost their momentum. Exact numbers are unavailable, but there is little doubt that there were fewer bands in America in 1920 than there had been in 1900. Now, in the 1980s, there are fewer still.

Bands continue to exist, of course. Wind ensembles, in which brass instruments are judiciously balanced with woodwinds, are popular formats for collegiate and professional music making. Many communities continue to allocate tax money for the traditional presentation of outdoor band concerts during the summer months, and some have even revitalized all-brass groups as a way of preserving the customs of the past. But the band movement as it was conceived and nurtured is gone. Bandstands, along with faded photographs and the occasional ode to a local band, are the most conspicuous and appealing relics of the movement that once touched the lives of almost everyone. ♪ ♪ ♪

THE GREAT BANDSTAND DESIGN COMPETITION

A BANDSTAND FOR OBERLIN

THEODORE LIEBMAN, FAIA

Oberlin, Ohio, a town of 9,000, is the home of Oberlin College, both a leading liberal arts and sciences college and a world-famous conservatory of music. At the center of Oberlin lies Tappan Square, a 13-acre village green owned by the college and open to all. It is the bucolic hub around which both college and town are clustered, a place where citizens and students alike participate in its activity and enjoy its beauty.

On three sides of the square are buildings of varied architectural styles—from Greek Revival to early post-Modern—including an Italian Renaissance art museum (1917) by Cass Gilbert with a 1977 addition by Robert Venturi. The fourth side contains a row of Italianate brick commercial buildings from the post–Civil War era as well as the neo-Gothic conservatory of music complex (1964) designed by Minoru Yamasaki. Tappan Square integrates this eclectic group of buildings into a pleasing whole.

The many towering trees on Tappan Square suggest rustic maturity, but once a half-dozen buildings occupied the square, which was turned into a village green early in the 20th century in accordance with the will of a wealthy alumnus, Charles Martin Hall. (Hall's research at Oberlin led to the discovery of the commercial process for producing aluminum metal; he later founded the Aluminum Company of America, now Alcoa.) A great admirer of open space, Hall's bequest required that the two remaining buildings on Tappan Square be removed to create a large open green area. The will, however, permitted the placement of small ornamental buildings in the square.

A bandstand had stood in a corner of the square from 1879 to 1907, when it was destroyed by fire. Geoffrey Blodgett, professor of history at Oberlin College, describes the early bandstand in his book, *Oberlin Architecture, College and Town:*

> In Oberlin, a small wooden bandstand on Tappan Square once helped to promote community vitality during the decades around the turn of the century. During eight months of the year for occasions that pulled together college people, townspeople and visitors, the bandstand served as a focus. Band concerts, vaudeville acts, minstrel shows, barber shop quartets, dramatic groups and Chautauqua speakers—often subsidized by either the College or village merchants—regularly drew large crowds.

THE COMPETITION PROCESS

To revive and stimulate public celebratory gatherings on a more regular basis, Oberlin College President S. Frederick Starr formed a bandstand advisory committee in 1983 to consider a new bandstand for Tappan Square. All members of the committee believed that

Oberlin College Band (1902–03), a 22-piece ensemble with a mixed brass and woodwind instrumentation. The years before World War I saw a gradual shift toward larger bands with clarinets and saxophones augmenting the brass and percussion. (Oberlin College Archives)

an international design competition could generate community involvement and would lead to an exciting and innovative structure.

The decision to hold such a competition is at once brilliant and incredibly difficult to implement: brilliant, in that it opens a dialogue to define the specific problem at hand and invites myriad solutions from a range of designers with varied philosophies and program interpretations; difficult, because the selection requires a consensus among a diversified group of jurors, each of whom has a special interest in some specific issue—generic, site specific, historical, social, ecological, practical or mystical.

Grover Mouton III, a New Orleans artist, worked with the committee to develop The Great Bandstand Design Competition project, which was eventually funded by the Design Arts Program of the National Endowment for the Arts in the fall of 1984. Oberlin College provided matching funds to carry out a design competition, open to all, and to award $5,000 for the winning design.

The bandstand competition's goal was to identify a structure for Tappan Square that would serve both ornamental and functional purposes. The bandstand could be of any style and was to accommodate from four to 40 musicians so that they could perform either during the day or at night and be given protection from sun, rain and wind. Specific site selection was left to the competitors. In addition, the design had to take into account the following needs:

1. To complement the highly variegated collection of buildings that surround the square.

2. To create an outdoor performance space for both the professional musicians of the college's conservatory of music and the community's musical organizations in order to enhance the ability of both college and community to hear and appreciate each other's musical offerings.

3. To provide a place to bring people together for a wide variety of college and town gatherings and celebrations.

In January 1985, the college announced the competition with the distribution of 12,000 colorful posters to art and architecture schools, architects, landscape architects, state arts councils and Oberlin alumni. The call for entries was listed in professional journals and the local and national press. Ultimately, 385 requests to enter were received from 37 states, Canada, Italy and France. Registration packages were mailed March 30, with submissions due May 8 for judging May 10-12. Before the official judging, 148 Oberlin bandstand entries from more than 30 states and several foreign countries were unwrapped and numbered, ensuring a blind competition. All were placed in one large auditorium so that the jury could at once view, review, ponder, discuss, eliminate, argue and finally select a winner. The rows of mounted drawings collectively represented untold hours of artistic labor and thought about the creation of a special bandstand in a special place.

The seven-member bandstand jury (see page 8) represented the fields of art, history, art history, music, musicology, architectural history, landscape architecture and architecture. Three of the jurors also knew the town intimately. The jury's discussions moved from site and design issues to practical accommodations of musical instruments, from the history of bandstands to architectural style, from a concert for a few to state-of-the-art sound technology. Over two full days, discussions by this special team of judges continuously defined and redefined the "simple" problem and slowly identified the solution.

On May 12 the winner was announced and the Oberlin community arrived with enthusiasm to view the exhibition of entries at the Allen Memorial Art Museum. Soon after, a second grant proposal to the NEA produced additional funds to assist in the publication of *The Oberlin Book of Bandstands* and to aid in preparing an exhibition of bandstand designs to travel across the country in 1987–88. In addition to the winning entry, 50 of the bandstand designs submitted to the competition are illustrated in the following pages.

Under the leadership of Oberlin President Starr and with the inspired and generous gift of an Oberlin resident, alumnus and contractor, A. H. Clark, less than two years after the jury convened to select the winning submission, the first-place bandstand design has become a reality.

The winning entry by Julian S. Smith probably could fit only in Oberlin, with its tradition of independent thought and its strong ties to Asia. It is at once a traditional Victorian bandstand in the style of wooden American architecture and a traditional Indian festival cart, sitting solidly on huge sandstone half wheels. A glimpse of it through the trees from different points on Tappan Square elicits delight and wonder: it will evoke endless discussion and provide infinite pleasure as it becomes part of the fabric of the community. ♪ ♪ ♪

THE OBERLIN BANDSTAND: UNRESTRICTED BY EUROPEAN IMAGERY

JULIAN S. SMITH

The challenge in designing a bandstand for Oberlin was to match the traditional elements of Victorian musical enterprise with the tendency of the Oberlin community to disregard traditional customs and prejudices. The decision to re-create a bandstand on Tappan Square had to be interpreted not as an exercise in nostalgia but as an attempt to explore how a long-overlooked medium might be used to open new channels for community expression and interaction.

In terms of architectural design, this meant taking a turn-of-the-century North American prototype and transforming it into a suitable contemporary vehicle for Oberlin's musical and educational pursuits. These pursuits are not limited by those based on classical European precedents. They increasingly encompass indigenous North American traditions and those of other cultures. It seemed that the architecture should be similarly unrestricted by European imagery.

The idea of a stage area defined by a perimeter colonnade, one frequently used in bandstand design, is derived from Europe but is rather restrictive as a form. Instead, I have used the heavy timber framing and decorative detailing of North American bandstand tradition to create a pavilion structure that in its broad overhanging roofs and large internal columns owes more to architectural traditions of the Far East. This form allowed a more flexible and intimate performance area. An access ramp was also easily integrated, as was the spreading masonry base, designed to lift the vulnerable wood structure out of the wet ground.

The half wheels carved out of the base, the yokelike aspect of the ramp and the general festival imagery extend the interplay between the static and the dynamic aspects of the bandstand tradition in general and of Oberlin's involvement with it in particular. Such imagery is intended to evoke the transient and often spontaneous nature of outdoor musical events. At the same time, the structure itself is designed to give that transience and spontaneity a focus that is relatively permanent and carefully crafted.

OBERLIN BANDSTAND DESIGNS

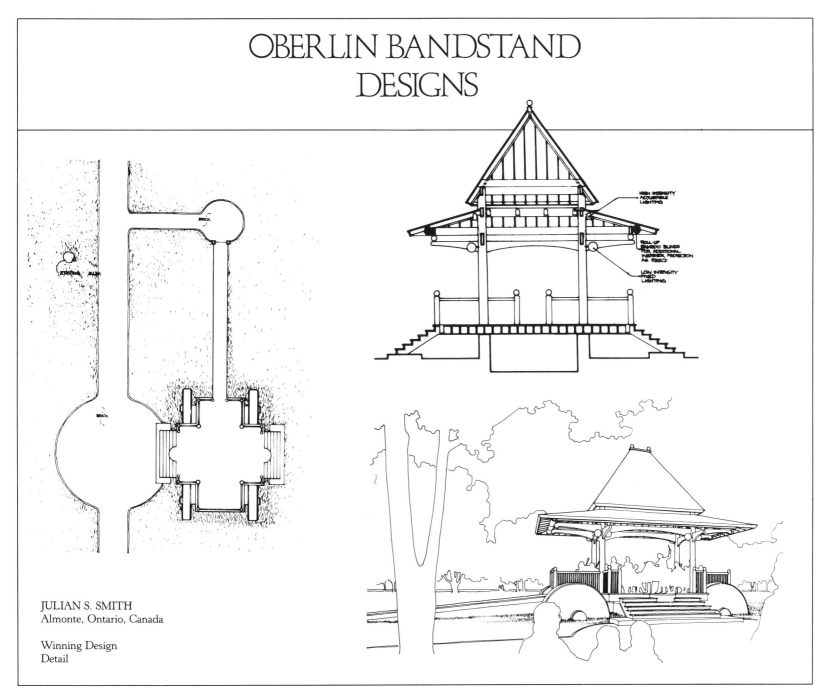

JULIAN S. SMITH
Almonte, Ontario, Canada

Winning Design
Detail

JAMES BRADBERRY
Philadelphia

Second Place (tie)
Detail

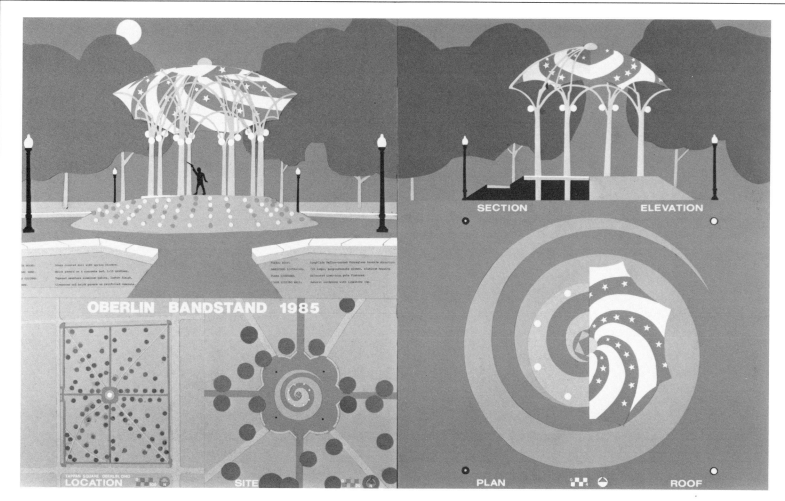

NAN LEGATE and ERIC FISS
Vancouver, British Columbia, Canada

Second Place (tie)

ASA ANDERSON/SCHWARTZ ARCHITECTS
Frederic Schwartz, partner in charge
Ross Anderson, Carolina Vacarro and Françoise Blanc
New York, San Francisco and Rome

Honorable Mention

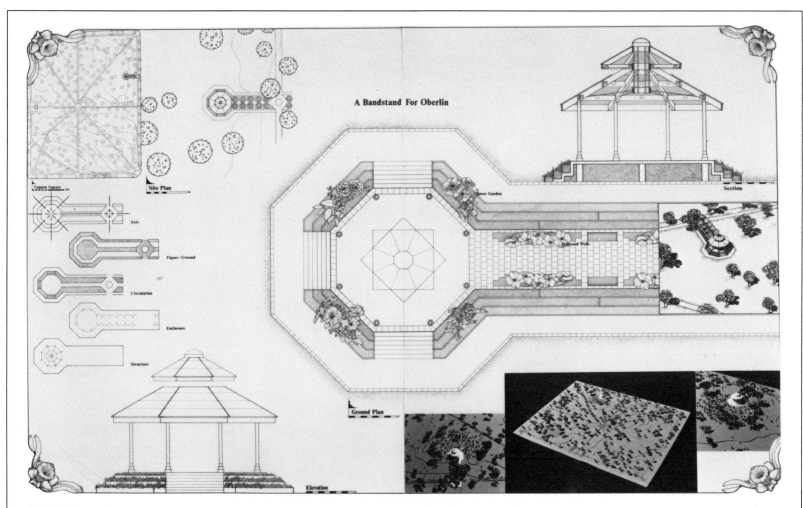

A Bandstand For Oberlin

DEWITT P. ZUSE III
New Haven, Conn.

Honorable Mention

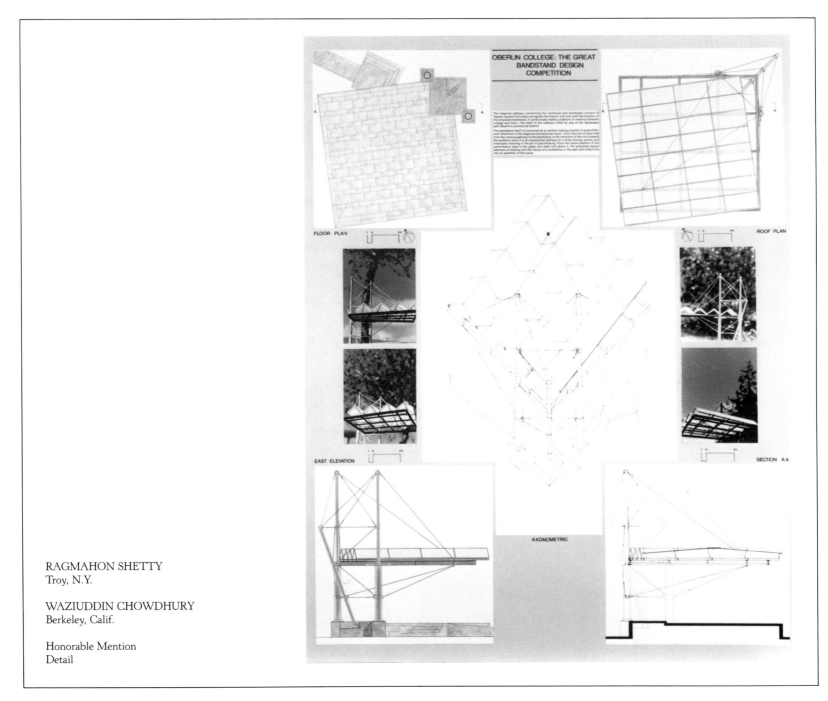

RAGMAHON SHETTY
Troy, N.Y.

WAZIUDDIN CHOWDHURY
Berkeley, Calif.

Honorable Mention
Detail

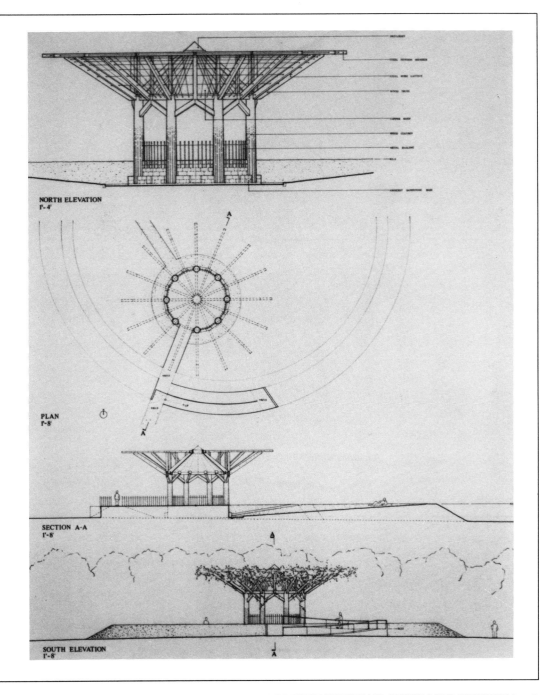

NORTH ELEVATION
1'-4'

PLAN
1'-8'

SECTION A-A
1'-8'

SOUTH ELEVATION
1'-8'

W. I. VAN CAMPEN
Syracuse, N.Y.

Honorable Mention
Detail

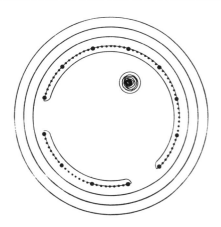

ROBERT B. WEISBORD
Wynnewood, Pa.

Honorable Mention
Detail

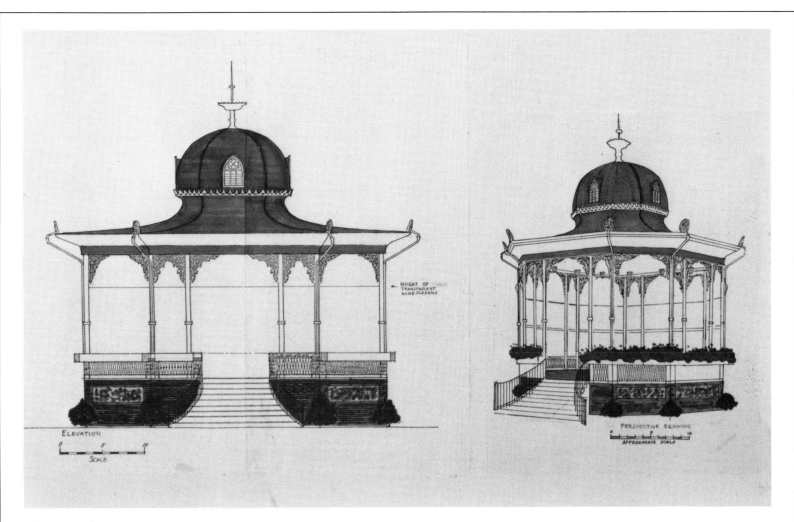

ROBERT M. STANTON
Madison, Wis.

Honorable Mention
Detail

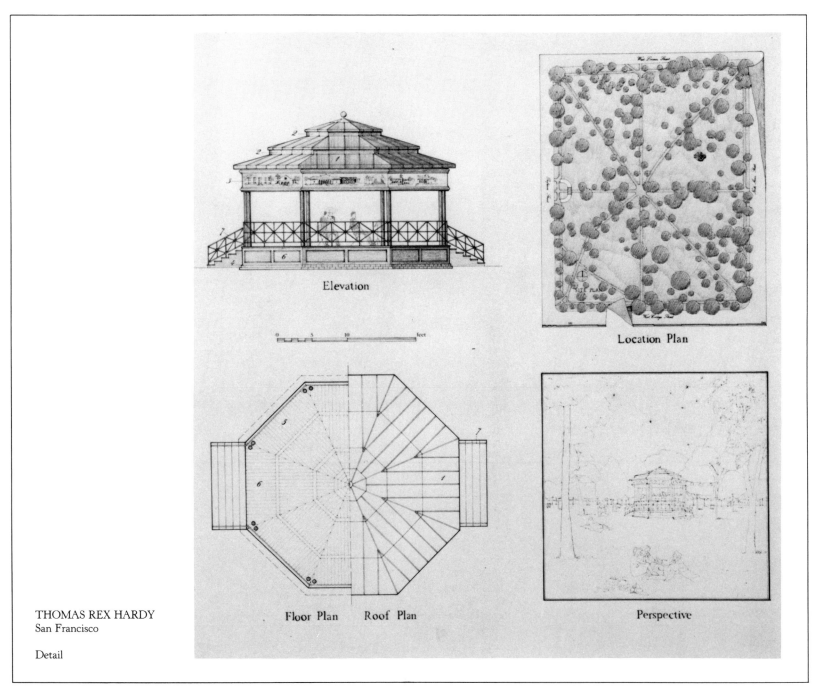

Elevation

Location Plan

Floor Plan   Roof Plan

Perspective

THOMAS REX HARDY
San Francisco

Detail

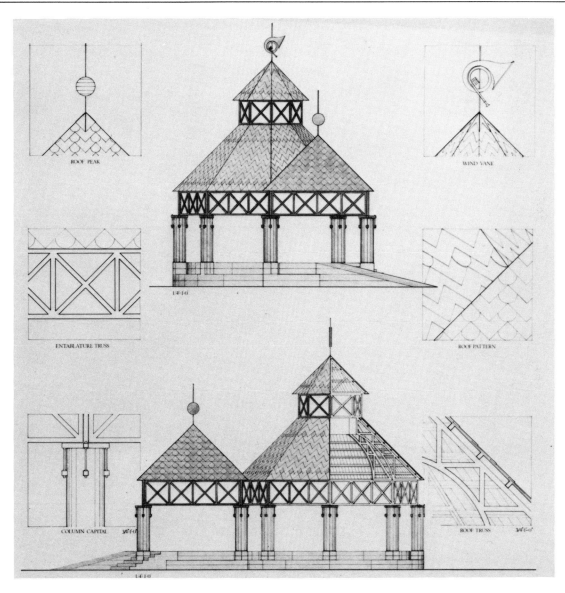

JAMES W. O'NEILL and DOUGLAS E. DICK
Cambridge, Mass.

Detail

CHARLES M. DITTO, LANDSCAPE ARCHITECT
Lima, Ohio

Detail

KARL D. BERG, R.A.
Berg Lewit Associates
New York City

Detail

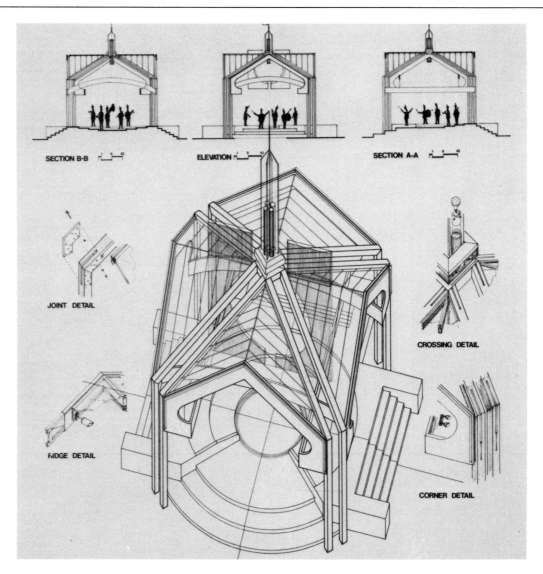

SECTION B-B

ELEVATION

SECTION A-A

JOINT DETAIL

CROSSING DETAIL

RIDGE DETAIL

CORNER DETAIL

KHOSROW BORZORGI and RICHARD FARLEY
Philadelphia

Detail

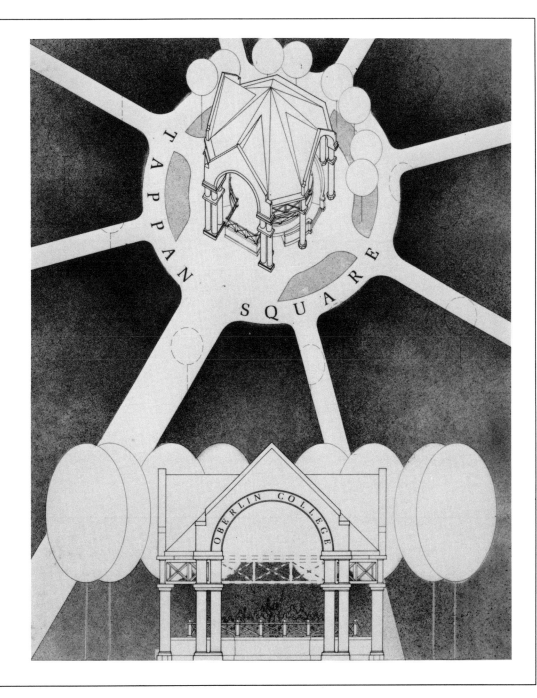

SEYFANG BLANCHARD ASSOCIATES, INC.
Robert A. Siebenaller, intern architect
Michael R. Duket, AIA
Toledo

Detail

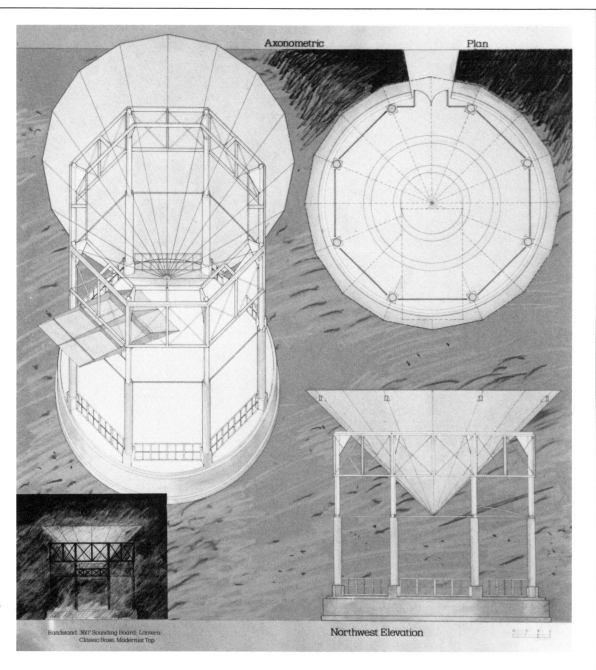

Axonometric

Plan

Bandstand: 360° Sounding Board; Lantern;
Classic Base, Modernist Top

Northwest Elevation

MARC TREIB and ANTONIO LAO
Berkeley, Calif.

Detail

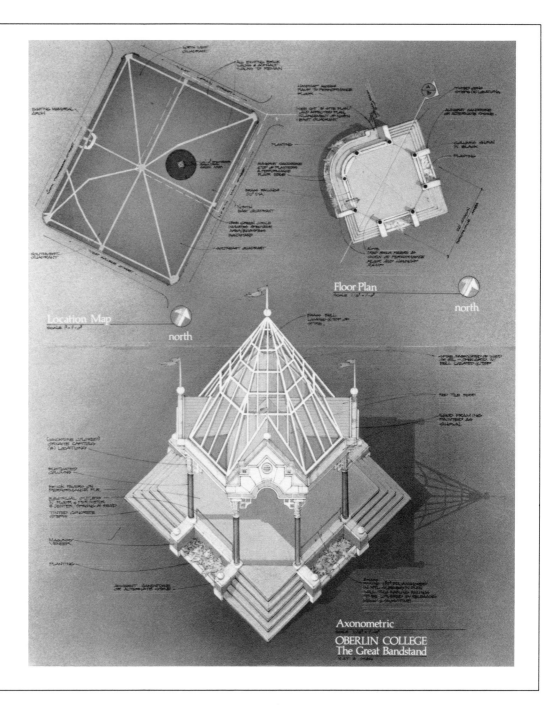

Location Map

Floor Plan

north

Axonometric

OBERLIN COLLEGE
The Great Bandstand

THOMAS McKAY FAIRCLOUGH
Salt Lake City

Detail

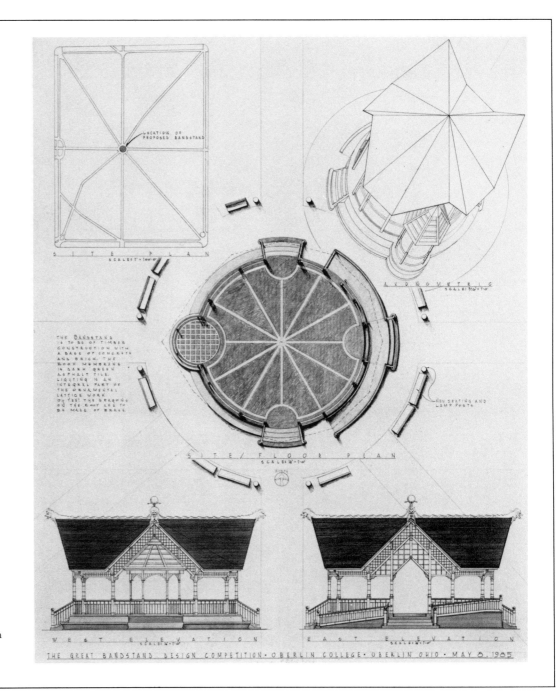

WILLIAM D. BAUNACH, architectural intern
Schmidt, Garden and Erickson, Inc.
Chicago

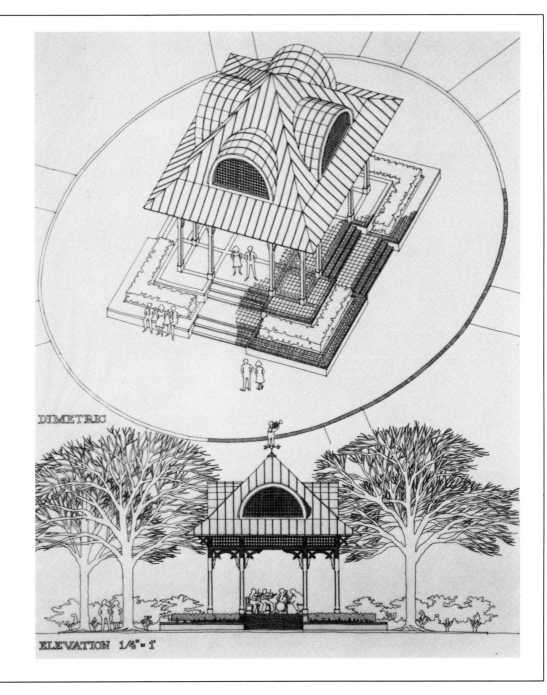

DIMETRIC

ELEVATION 1/4" = 1'

JOHN R. REITER, AIA, ARCHITECT
Savannah

Detail

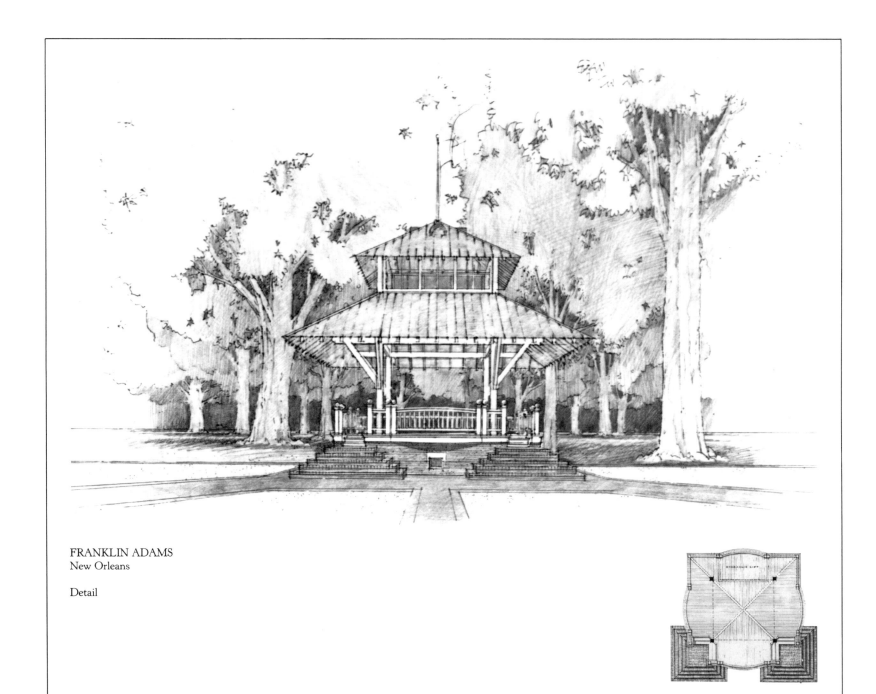

FRANKLIN ADAMS
New Orleans

Detail

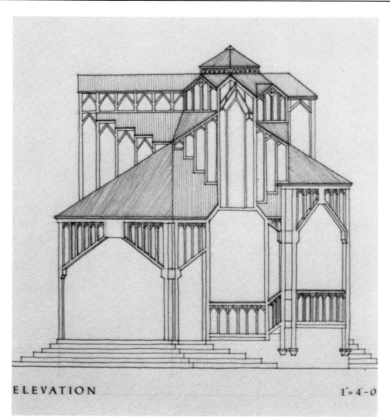

ELEVATION   1"=4'-0"

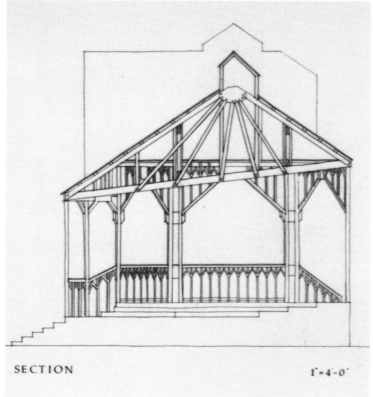

SECTION   1"=4'-0"

CHARLES W. MOORE, FAIA
Charles W. Moore, Arthur W. Anderson and Paul M. Lamb
Austin

Detail

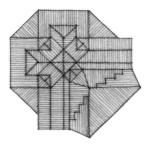

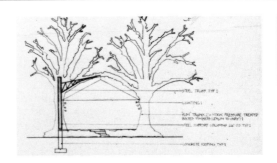

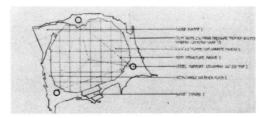

CAROL HENDERSON, designer and renderer
New Haven, Conn.

CHARLIE HUSEY, renderer
New York City

Detail

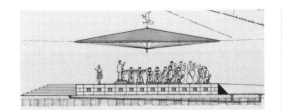

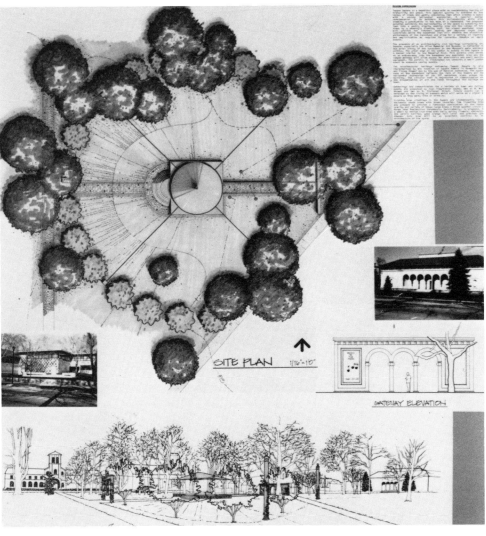

SITE PLAN

GATEWAY ELEVATION

WALTER KEHM and BRAD KEELER
Toronto, Ontario, Canada

Detail

NORTH ELEVATION   0 5 10

EAST ELEVATION   10 5 0

KATHLEEN M. O'MEARA
Boston

ENGELHARDT DESIGN
William R. Engelhardt and Bayard Engelhardt
Minneapolis

Detail

VIEW LOOKING SOUTHEAST

DAVID R. HECHT, student intern
Shaughnessy Fickel and Scott Architects Inc.
Kansas City, Mo.

Detail

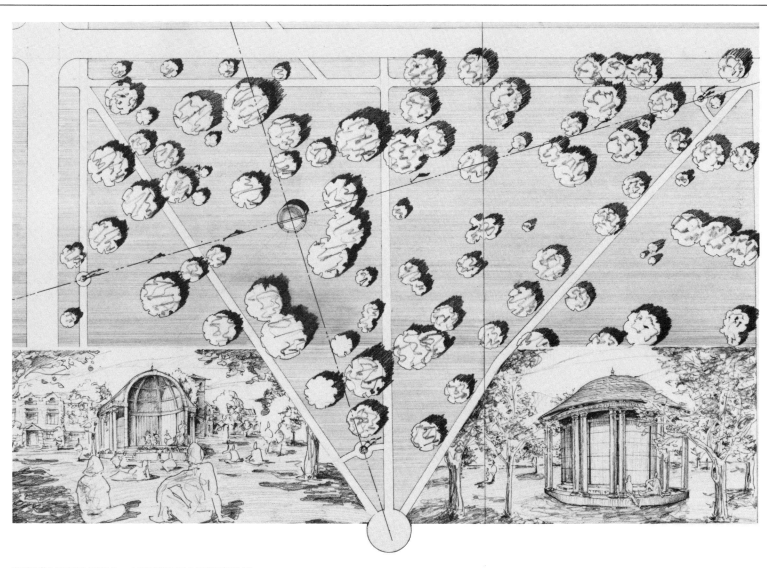

DENISE HARADEM and JEFFREY J. LOUSTAU
San Francisco

Detail

BRYAN R. CANNON
Washington, D.C.

Detail

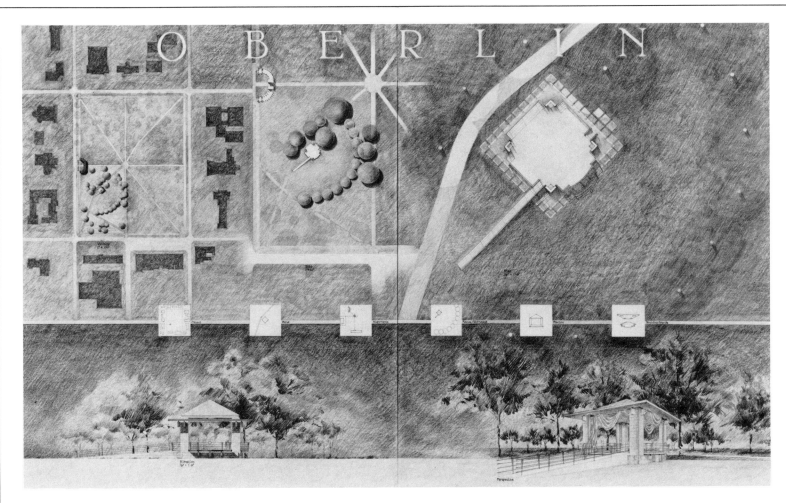

RAYMOND STREETER and LATHAM SHINDER
Manhattan, Kans.

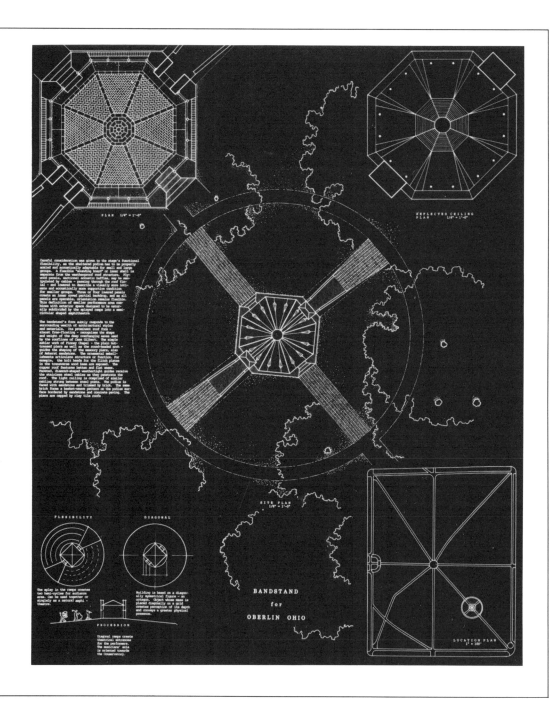

HILLARY BROWN AND
DEMETRI SARANTITIS, ARCHITECTS
Ting-I Kang
New York City

Detail

REGINALD MALCOLMSON
Ann Arbor, Mich.

Detail

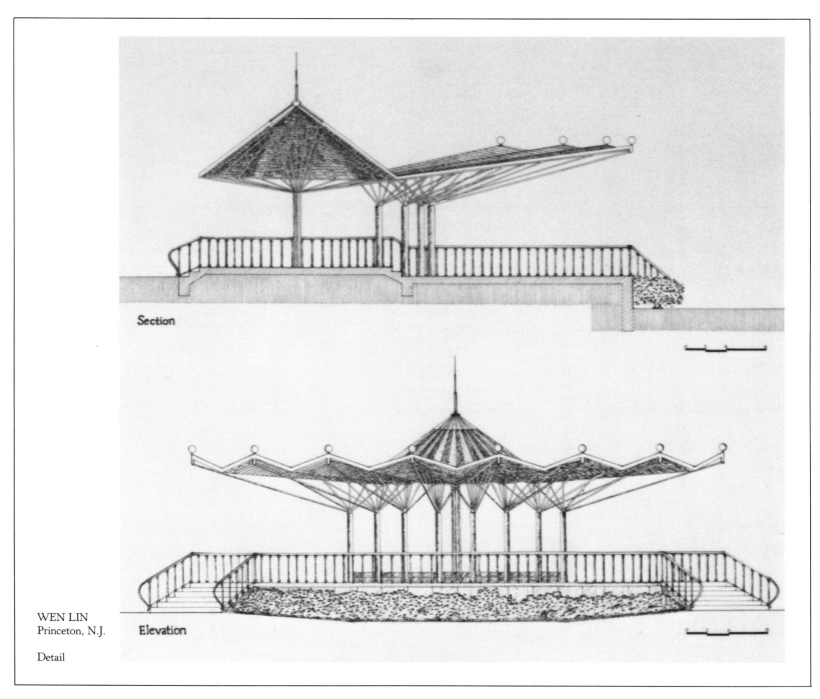

Section

Elevation

WEN LIN
Princeton, N.J.

Detail

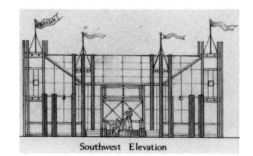

Southwest Elevation

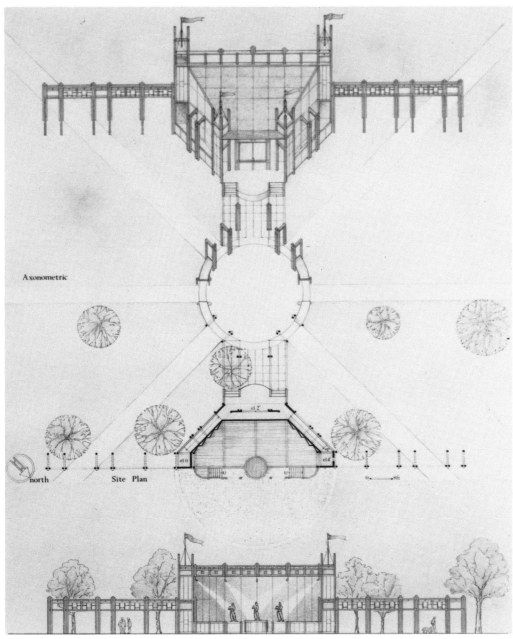

Axonometric

north   Site Plan

KAREN VAN LENGEN and WENDY EVANS
New York City

Detail

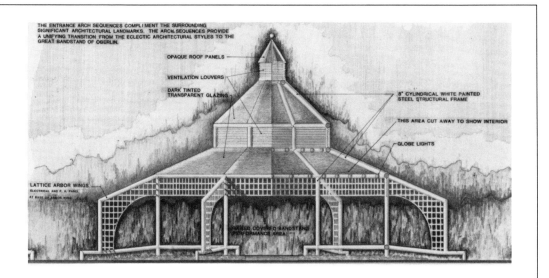

THE ENTRANCE ARCH SEQUENCES COMPLIMENT THE SURROUNDING
SIGNIFICANT ARCHITECTURAL LANDMARKS. THE ARCH SEQUENCES PROVIDE
A UNIFYING TRANSITION FROM THE ECLECTIC ARCHITECTURAL STYLES TO THE
GREAT BANDSTAND OF OBERLIN.

OPAQUE ROOF PANELS

VENTILATION LOUVERS

DARK TINTED
TRANSPARENT GLAZING

8" CYLINDRICAL WHITE PAINTED
STEEL STRUCTURAL FRAME

THIS AREA CUT AWAY TO SHOW INTERIOR

GLOBE LIGHTS

LATTICE ARBOR WINGS
ELECTRICAL AND P. A. PANEL
AT BASE OF ARBOR WINGS

COVERED BANDSTAND
PERFORMANCE AREA

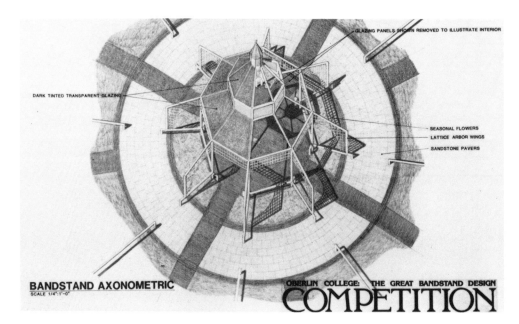

GLAZING PANELS SHOWN REMOVED TO ILLUSTRATE INTERIOR

DARK TINTED TRANSPARENT GLAZING

SEASONAL FLOWERS

LATTICE ARBOR WINGS

SANDSTONE PAVERS

BANDSTAND AXONOMETRIC
SCALE 1/4":1'-0"

OBERLIN COLLEGE: THE GREAT BANDSTAND DESIGN
COMPETITION

T. C. ARCHITECTS INCORPORATED
Robert Chordar, Scott D. Lukens and
David W. Fenn, AIA, principal
Akron

Detail

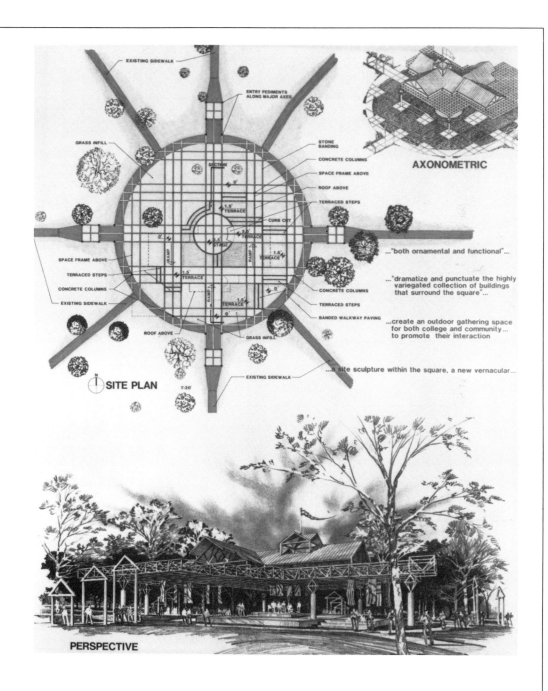

AXONOMETRIC

SITE PLAN

...EXISTING SIDEWALK

ENTRY PEDIMENTS
ALONG MAJOR AXES

GRASS INFILL

STONE
BANDING

CONCRETE COLUMNS

SPACE FRAME ABOVE

ROOF ABOVE

TERRACED STEPS

CURB CUT

SPACE FRAME ABOVE

TERRACED STEPS

CONCRETE COLUMNS

EXISTING SIDEWALK

CONCRETE COLUMNS

TERRACED STEPS

BANDED WALKWAY PAVING

ROOF ABOVE

GRASS INFILL

EXISTING SIDEWALK

..."both ornamental and functional"...

..."dramatize and punctuate the highly
variegated collection of buildings
that surround the square"...

...create an outdoor gathering space
for both college and community...
to promote their interaction

...a site sculpture within the square, a new vernacular...

PERSPECTIVE

CHERYL D. MOORE and
MICHAEL R. WEST, project designers
Dudley M. Fleming, perspective drawing
Richmond, Va.

Detail

GARZ/PESCH ARCHITECTS
Michael D. Garz and Maarten I. Pesch
Philadelphia

ORNAMENTAL SIGNATURE PLATES

NAMES OF D   ONORS INSC   RIBED HERE

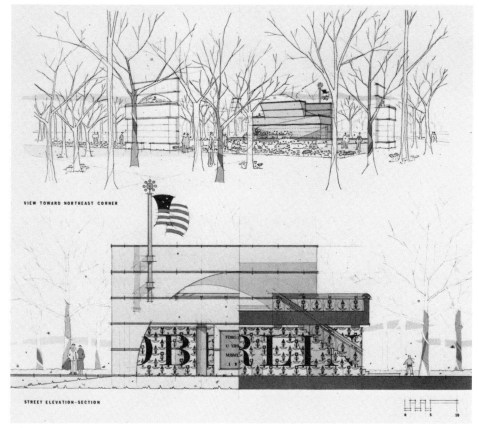

VIEW TOWARD NORTHEAST CORNER

STREET ELEVATION-SECTION

MATTHEW J. SCHOTTELKOTTE
Muller and Brown Architects
Cincinnati

Detail

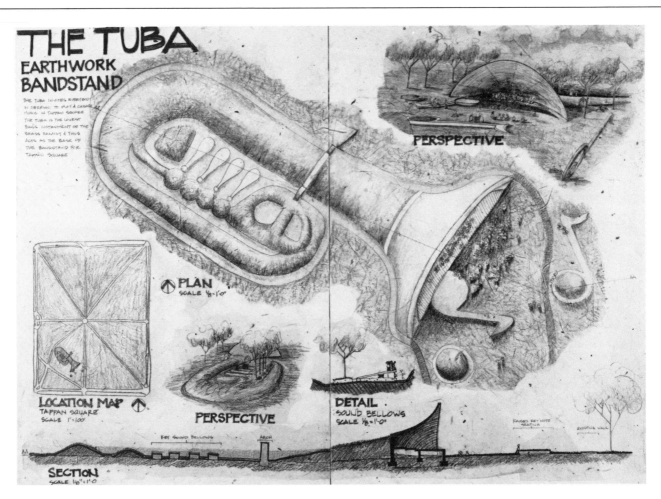

ANNE B. STAMPER
Seattle

Detail

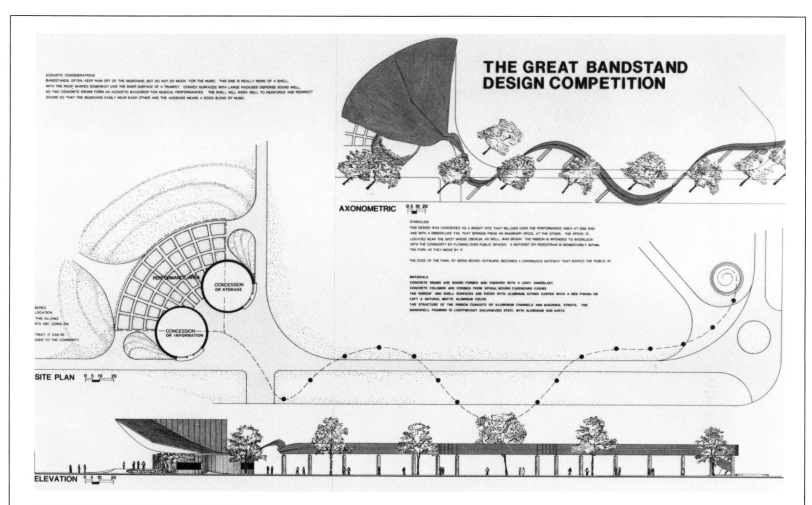

THE GREAT BANDSTAND DESIGN COMPETITION

BAUER, STARK AND LASHBROOK INC.
Charles H. Stark III, Paul Sullivan and Tim Bailey
Toledo

Detail

STANLEY MATHEWS
Oberlin, Ohio

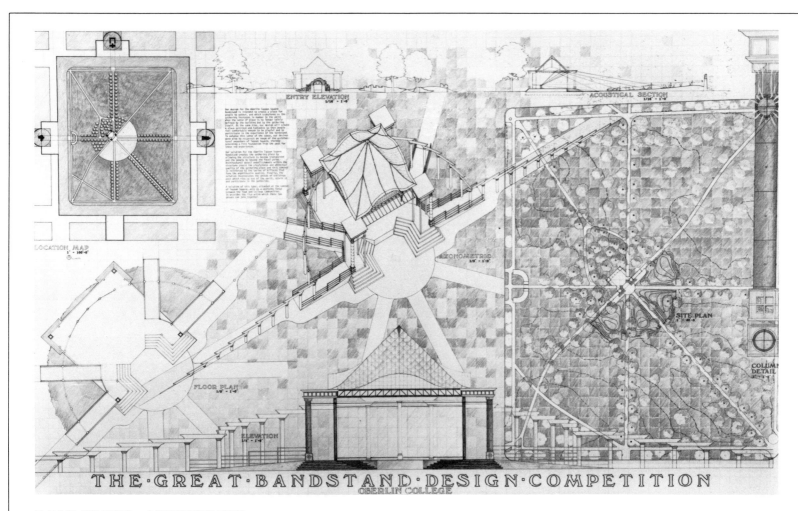

AMALIA IGLESIAS and SCOTT WEAVER
Columbus, Ohio

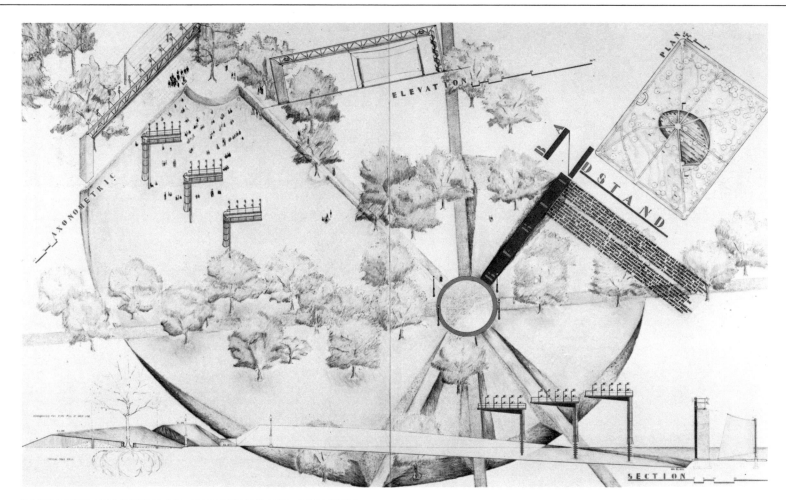

WURMFELD ASSOCIATES, P.C., ARCHITECTS AND ENGINEERS
Michael Wurmfeld, Robert Hart, Michael Cranfill and Charles Wurmfeld

DANIEL D. STEWART AND ASSOCIATES, LANDSCAPE ARCHITECTS
Daniel D. Stewart and Donald Walsh
New York City

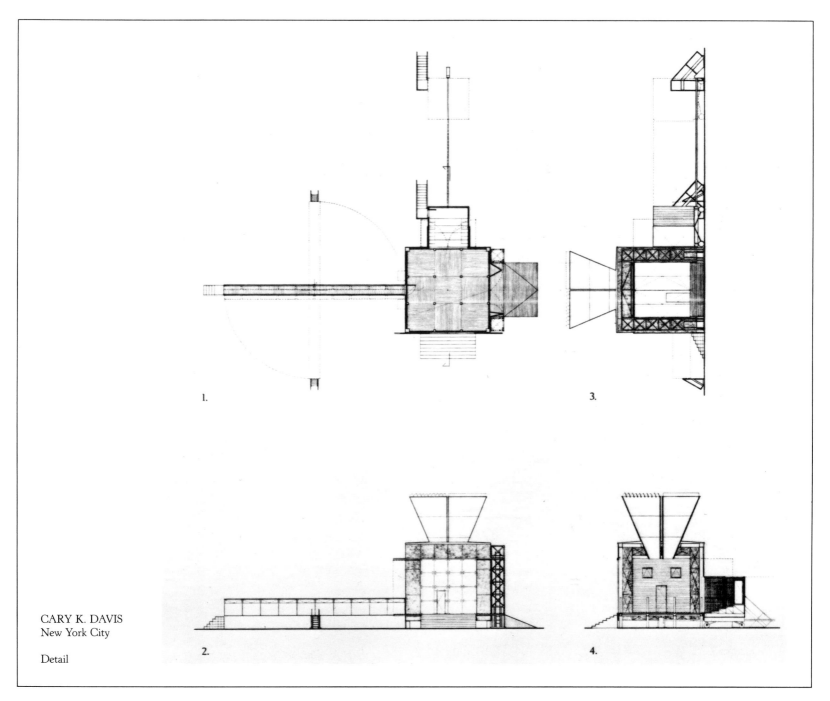

CARY K. DAVIS
New York City

Detail

1.

2.

3.

4.

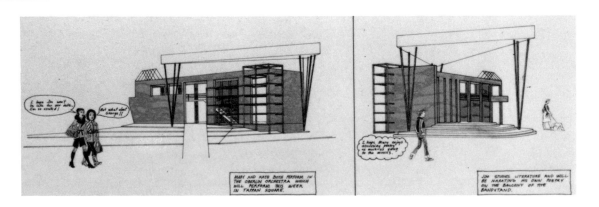

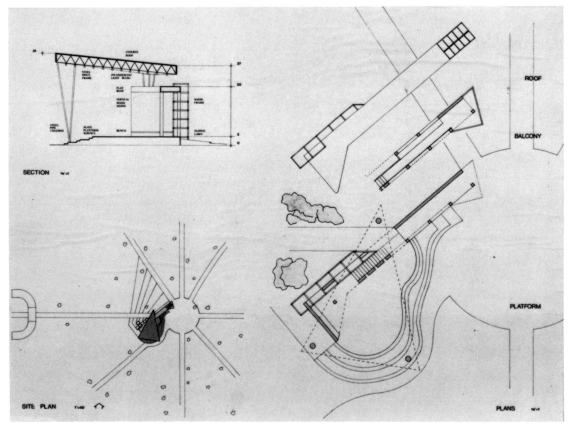

PETER COUWENBERGH
New York City

Detail

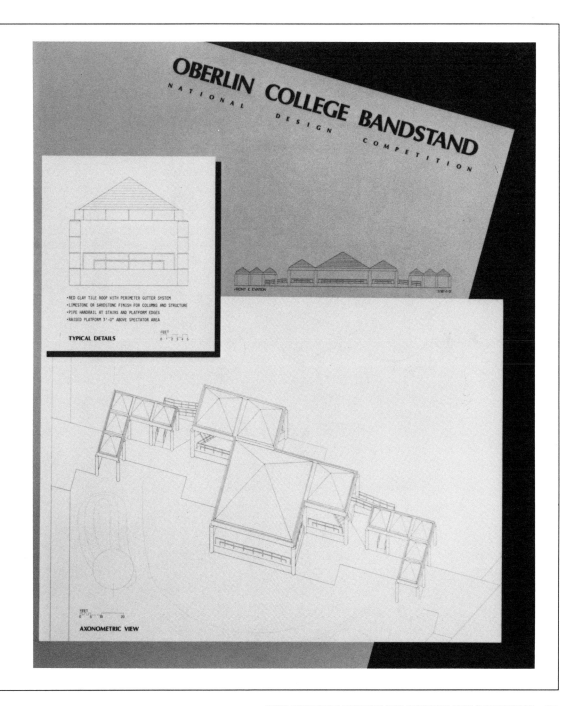

RICHARD PETER KRALY, AIA, CSI
Cleveland

Detail

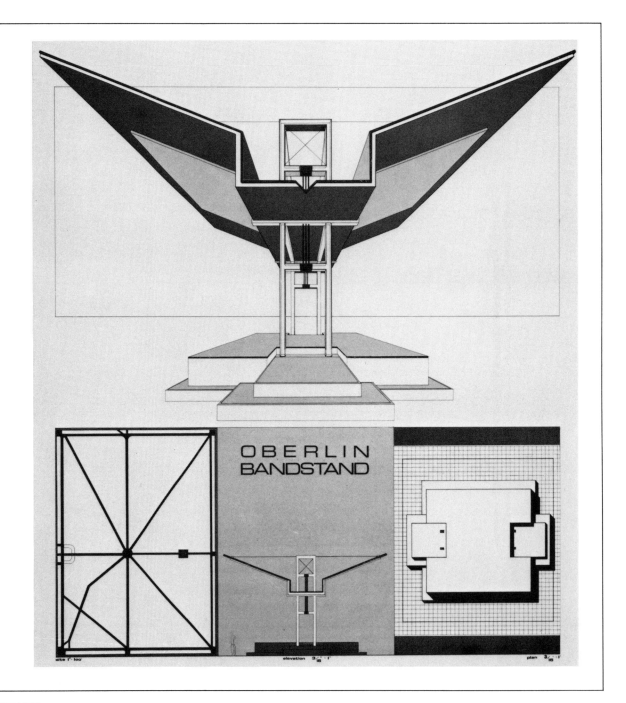

OBERLIN
BANDSTAND

JAY DAVID KAMMEN
San Francisco

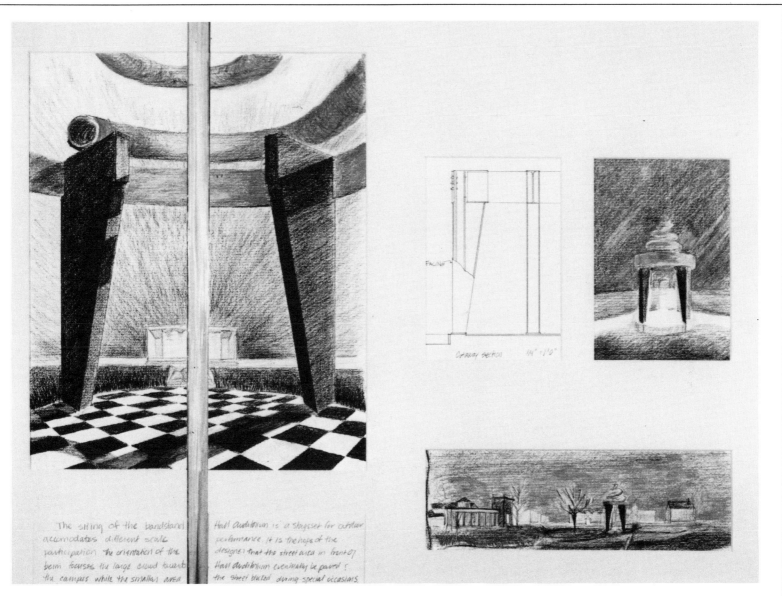

The siting of the bandstand accomodates different scale participation the orientation of the berm focuses the large cloud towards the campus while the smaller area

Hall Auditorium is a stage set for outdoor performance. It is the hope of the designer that the street area in front of Hall Auditorium eventually be paved & the street closed during special occasions

SUSAN H. PAPADAKIS
New Haven, Conn.

Detail

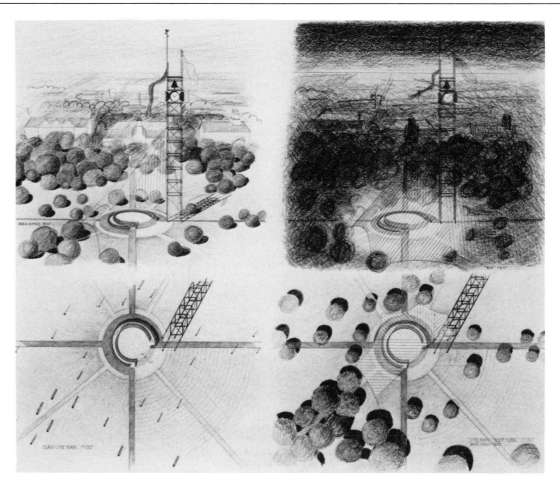

JAN S. KALINOWSKI, ARCHITECT
Bronx, N.Y.

Detail

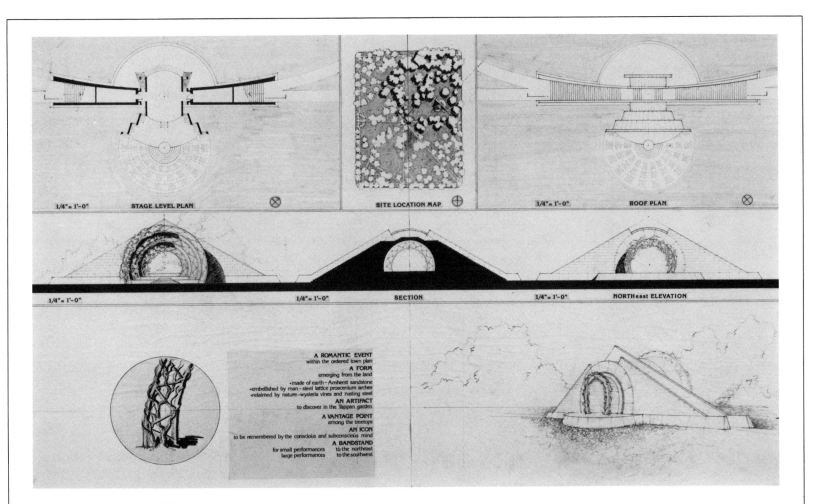

1/4" = 1'-0"   1/4" = 1'-0"   SECTION   1/4" = 1'-0"   NORTHeast ELEVATION

A ROMANTIC EVENT
within the ordered town plan
A FORM
emerging from the land
•made of earth – Amherst sandstone
•embellished by man – steel lattice proscenium arches
•reclaimed by nature – wysteria vines and rusting steel
AN ARTIFACT
to discover in the Tappan garden
A VANTAGE POINT
among the treetops
AN ICON
to be remembered by the conscious and subconscious mind
A BANDSTAND
for small performances   to the northeast
large performances   to the southwest

GILVARG EPSTEIN DESIGN
Eric W. Epstein, partner in charge
R. Anthony Terry, project designer
Bahman Negahban and David Must, project team
New Haven, Conn.

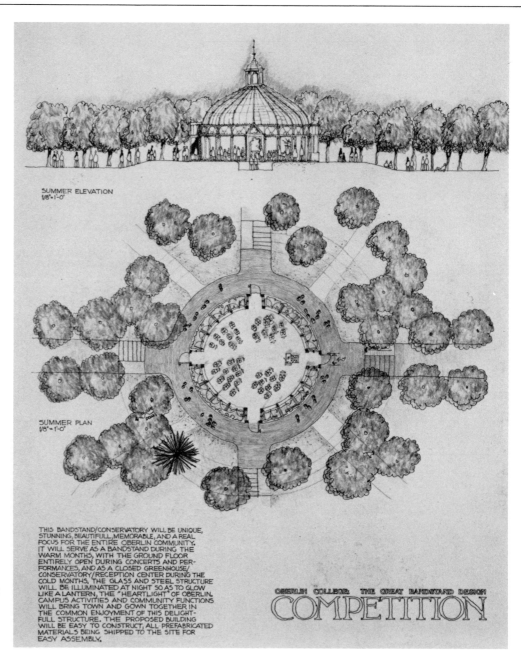

SUMMER ELEVATION
1/8" = 1'-0"

SUMMER PLAN
1/8" = 1'-0"

THIS BANDSTAND/CONSERVATORY WILL BE UNIQUE, STUNNING, BEAUTIFULL, MEMORABLE, AND A REAL FOCUS FOR THE ENTIRE OBERLIN COMMUNITY. IT WILL SERVE AS A BANDSTAND DURING THE WARM MONTHS, WITH THE GROUND FLOOR ENTIRELY OPEN DURING CONCERTS AND PERFORMANCES, AND AS A CLOSED GREENHOUSE/CONSERVATORY/RECEPTION CENTER DURING THE COLD MONTHS. THE GLASS AND STEEL STRUCTURE WILL BE ILLUMINATED AT NIGHT SO AS TO GLOW LIKE A LANTERN, THE "HEARTLIGHT" OF OBERLIN. CAMPUS ACTIVITIES AND COMMUNITY FUNCTIONS WILL BRING TOWN AND GOWN TOGETHER IN THE COMMON ENJOYMENT OF THIS DELIGHTFULL STRUCTURE. THE PROPOSED BUILDING WILL BE EASY TO CONSTRUCT, ALL PREFABRICATED MATERIALS BEING SHIPPED TO THE SITE FOR EASY ASSEMBLY.

OBERLIN COLLEGE: THE GREAT BANDSTAND DESIGN
COMPETITION

ROGER C. ERICKSON, senior landscape architect
PAM SCHOOLEY, landscape designer
Watertown, Mass.

Detail

MARK ZAHNER
Shawnee Mission, Kans.

Detail

PARTIAL LIST OF COMPETITION ENTRANTS

(not illustrated)

RICHARD C. ALVORD
West Roxbury, Mass.

HAMID ASHKI and RUNE FORBERG
Lexington, Ky.

BUILDING TYPES—ARCHITECTS
Walter Boykowycz and Kathy Boykowycz
Pittsburgh

STEVE CAVANAUGH, JOHN CINELLI and KURT LORENZ
Champaign, Ill.

DENNIS KEITH COWART and SONIA McNABB-COWART
New Orleans

ERIC DOEPKE ASSOCIATES
Eric Doepke, James T. Kalsbeek and Stephen A. Smith
Cincinnati

GASTON EUBANKS and WHITEFIELD NEILL
The Tulane Architectural Coalition
New Orleans

PETER FORBES ASSOCIATES
Peter Forbes, Elizabeth S. Nemura, David Tobias and Bradford C. Walker
Boston

MITCHELL GANTZ
The Preservation Partnership
New Bedford, Mass.

LAND CORRIDORS
Marsha Effron Barron, Jacqueline Ignon and Thomas A. Lockett
Palos Verdes Estates, Calif.

MARIO MADAYAG
New York City

KEITH MILLAY and SYBIL FICKETT-JONES
Boston

ALAN M. ROSS, ERLYNNE KITAGAWA and SARA JOHNSTON
Broadstreet Design Group
Boston

STEVEN CLAIR SHAFFER
Bloomsburg, Pa.

RUSSELL SWANSON
Princeton, N.J.

CLINTON J. D. TERRY
Berkeley, Calif.

ALLAN WEXLER and ELLEN WEXLER
New York City

McKinley monument and bandstand (c. 1895; demolished), Blairsville, Pa. (Lake County Museum, Curt Teich Postcard Collection)

FURTHER READING
♪ ♪ ♪

"The Bandstand," *Selmer Bandwagon* 92 (1980): 10–13

Barlow, Elizabeth, with illustrations by William Alex. *Frederick Law Olmsted's New York.* New York: Frederick A. Praeger, 1972.

Blodgett, Geoffrey. *Oberlin Architecture, College and Town: A Guide to Its Social History.* Kent, Ohio: Kent State University Press, 1985.

Downing, Andrew Jackson. *A Treatise on the Theory and Practice of Landscape Gardening.* New York: C. M. Saxton, 1855. Reprint. New York: Funk, 1967; Little Compton, R.I.: Theophrastus, 1981.

Forsythe, Michael. *Buildings for Music: The Architect, the Musician, and the Listener from the 17th Century to the Present Day.* Cambridge, Mass.: MIT Press, 1985.

Girouard, Mark. *Cities and People: A Social and Architectural Guide.* New Haven, Conn.: Yale University Press, 1985.

Hazen, Margaret Hindle, and Robert M. Hazen. *The Music Men.* Washington, D.C.: Smithsonian Institution Press, 1987.

Jackson, John Brinckerhoff. *American Space: The Centennial Years, 1865–1876.* New York: W. W. Norton, 1972.

Kelly, Bruce, Gail Travis Guillet and Mary Ellen W. Hern. *Art of the Olmsted Landscape.* New York: Landmarks Preservation Commission of New York City, 1981.

Olmsted, Frederick Law, Jr., and Theodora Kimball, eds. *Frederick Law Olmsted: Landscpe Architect, 1822–1903.* 1922. Reprint. New York: Benjamin Blom, 1970.

Robinson, Charles Mulford. *The Improvement of Towns and Cities.* 3rd ed. New York: G. P. Putnam's Sons, 1907.

————. *Modern Civic Art, or The City Made Beautiful.* 4th ed. New York: G. P. Putnam's Sons, 1918.

Stein, Susan R., ed. *The Architecture of Richard Morris Hunt.* Chicago: University of Chicago Press, 1986.

Strombeck, Janet H., and Richard H. Strombeck. *Gazebos and Other Garden Structures.* Delafield, Wis.: Sun Designs, 1983.

Vaux, Calvert. *Villas and Cottages.* New York: Harper and Brothers, 1857. Reprint. New York: Dover Publications, 1970.

Band shell (c. 1900), Eureka Springs, Ark., still attracting crowds to music concerts, including jazz festivals. (Lake County Museum, Curt Teich Postcard Collection)

INDEX

♪ ♪ ♪

Bandstands and other sites are listed under their town or city locations. Page numbers in italics refer to illustrations and captions.

AUTHORS
♪ ♪ ♪

CHARLES GWATHMEY, FAIA, principal architect of Gwathmey Siegel and Associates Architects, New York City, developed the design program of Oberlin College's new North Campus dining and social facility in 1987. In the 18 years of his association with Robert Siegel, the firm has won 50 design awards for residential and institutional designs, including the interior reconstruction of Princeton University's Whig Hall and the student union facility at the State University of New York (SUNY) at Purchase, N.Y.

S. FREDERICK STARR, 12th president of Oberlin College, has written three books and more than 20 articles on the history of architecture and city planning and is currently developing a volume on the architecture and social history of New Orleans's Garden District. Before accepting the presidency of Oberlin in 1983, he served as vice president for academic affairs at Tulane University in New Orleans, where he also founded the Louisiana Repertory Jazz Ensemble, an eight-member group that continues to perform and record classical jazz. Starr also is a leading authority on the USSR and was founding secretary of the Kennan Institute for Advanced Russian Studies at the Smithsonian Institution's Wilson Center in Washington, D.C.

MARGARET HINDLE HAZEN is a professional researcher, librarian, historian and writer on subjects such as songs of revolutionary America and the history of American mineral industries. Her book, *The Music Men: An Illustrated History of Brass Bands in America, 1800–1920* (Smithsonian Institution Press, 1987), was written with her husband, Robert M. Hazen, a professional symphonic trumpeter. Using their extensive collection of band ephemera, including photographs, programs, picture postcards and advertisements, they chronicled the band movement in the context of American society at large. Hazen is currently serving as a consultant to the archives of the National Museum of American History of the Smithsonian Institution.

THEODORE LIEBMAN, FAIA, of the Liebman Melting Partnership, Architects and Planners, New York City, has long been associated with the design of major affordable housing and neighborhood development programs. The firm has developed strategies for urban development, historical restoration and certification, adaptive use of old structures, creative research in housing and architectural technology, and the behavioral and cultural aspects of new communities and neighborhoods. Liebman is a fellow of the American Academy in Rome.

JULIAN S. SMITH, winner of the Oberlin bandstand design competition, was until recently chief architect for Canada's National Historic Parks and Sites program. He now maintains an architectural practice in Ottawa, Ontario. After being graduated from Oberlin College in 1969, Smith, an accomplished violinist, lived in India for two years studying Indian architecture and classical music. While there he became fascinated with festival processions, an interest reflected in his design for Oberlin's new bandstand. He holds a master's degree in architecture from the Massachusetts Institute of Technology.

Concert in 1886 at the bandstand (c. 1885; demolished) in Horton Plaza, San Diego. Here listeners extended the seating arrangement with horses and buggies. (Title Insurance and Trust Company, San Diego)

OTHER BOOKS FROM THE PRESERVATION PRESS

♪ ♪ ♪

Building Watchers Series

WHAT STYLE IS IT? A GUIDE TO AMERICAN ARCHITECTURE. John Poppeliers, S. Allen Chambers, Jr., and Nancy B. Schwartz, Historic American Buildings Survey. One of the most popular, concise books on American architectural styles, this portable guidebook is designed for easy identification of 22 styles of buildings at home or on the road. 112 pp., illus., biblio., gloss. $7.95 pb.

MASTER BUILDERS: A GUIDE TO FAMOUS AMERICAN ARCHITECTS. Introduction by Roger K. Lewis. Forty major architects who have left indelible marks on American architecture—from Bulfinch to Venturi—are profiled in this entertaining introduction. 204 pp., illus., biblio., append., index. $9.95 pb.

BUILT IN THE U.S.A.: AMERICAN BUILDINGS FROM AIRPORTS TO ZOOS. Diane Maddex, Editor. A guidebook-sized history of 42 American building types, showing how their forms developed from their functions. 192 pp., illus., biblio., append. $9.95 pb.

AMERICA'S ARCHITECTURAL ROOTS: ETHNIC GROUPS THAT BUILT AMERICA. Dell Upton, Editor. Ethnic groups from Africans to Ukrainians have shaped the way our buildings look. Highlighted here are 22 groups, featured in heavily illustrated chapters that document the rich ethnic diversity of American architecture. 196 pp., illus., biblio., index. $9.95 pb.

THE BUILDINGS OF MAIN STREET: A GUIDE TO AMERICAN COMMERCIAL ARCHITECTURE. Richard Longstreth. A fresh look at architecture found along America's Main Streets. Building types are documented in this unique guide with 220 illustrations from towns and cities across the country. 156 pp., illus., biblio., index. $8.95 pb.

ALL ABOUT OLD BUILDINGS: THE WHOLE PRESERVATION CATALOG. Diane Maddex, Editor. This fact-filled book offers a lively, readable mixture of illustrations, sources of help, case histories, excerpts and quotations on 15 major subject areas. 436 pp., illus., biblio., index. $39.95 hb, $24.95 pb.

AMERICA'S CITY HALLS. William L. Lebovich, Historic American Buildings Survey. Two centuries of municipal architecture are captured in this book featuring 500 photographs of 114 city halls in 40 states. 224pp., illus., biblio., append., indexes. $18.95 pb.

AMERICA'S COUNTRY SCHOOLS. Andrew Gulliford. Captures the historical and architectural legacy of country schools from soddies and frame buildings to octagons and provides ideas for preserving them. 296 pp., illus., append., index. $18.95 pb.

GOODBYE HISTORY, HELLO HAMBURGER: AN ANTHOLOGY OF ARCHITECTURAL DELIGHTS AND DISASTERS. Ada Louise Huxtable. Foreword by John B. Oakes. These 68 pieces, most originally published by the *New York Times,* cover the classic urban confrontations of the 1960s and 1970s, analyzing the failures and successes and urging us to create more livable cities. 208 pp., illus., index. $14.95 pb.

GREAT AMERICAN BRIDGES AND DAMS. Donald C. Jackson. The first guide to 300 of the most important and best-known bridges and dams in the Untied States. Organized by region, state and location, the guide includes historical, engineering and architectural information on each bridge and dam, provides an overview of the history of these endangered structures and discusses preservation issues involved in saving them. Great American Places Series. 300 pp., illus., biblio., append., index. $16.95 pb.

GREAT AMERICAN MOVIE THEATERS. David Naylor. The first guide to 360 of the most dazzling and historic movie theaters still standing throughout the country. Organized by region, state and city, the entries provide colorful architectural and historical descriptions of these magnificent landmarks. An essay details preservation problems—and solutions—while a coda brings back some of the lost great theaters for a final call. Great American Places Series. 276 pp., illus., biblio., index. $16.95 pb.

To order Preservation Press books, send the total of the book prices (less 10 percent discount for National Trust members), plus $3 postage and handling, to: Mail Order, National Trust for Historic Preservation, 1600 H Street, N.W., Washington, D.C. 20006. Residents of California, Colorado, Washington, D.C., Illinois, Iowa, Louisiana, Maryland, Massachusetts, New York, Pennsylvania, South Carolina, Texas and Virginia please add applicable sales tax. Make checks payable to the National Trust or provide credit card number, expiration date, signature and telephone number.